About the Author

Tessa is a career and executive coach, specialised in aiding professionals who have lost their jobs or face health issues. Her INNERPULSE coaching programs help them to find purpose and regain well-being, as well as to perform at the highest level.

Before starting to work in the business arena, Tessa was a professional classical musician, performing at a high international level, composing and teaching for more than 30 years. During this time, she travelled the outer and inner worlds, exploring and developing practices that help to perform at the top level while simultaneously safeguarding one's inner balance and well-being. These include forms of meditation, autogenic training, shamanism and mindset techniques used by top athletes. In her second career as a professional artist, during which time her work was exhibited and sold internationally, she learned how images convey information and energy, how they have a profound impact on us, and how we can use them to our advantage in times of crisis and when facing challenges.

Having successfully changed careers and built several of her own businesses, she has now become a sought-after coach for outplacement or business people of all levels, from C-level to highly trained specialists. Her experience working with professionals in crises, as well as her own healing from major and minor illnesses, using the tools and processes developed over the course of her life have led her to see the strong correlation between living one's purpose, health and top performance.

Tessa is a tree hugger and enjoys swimming in lakes as soon as the sun comes out.

INNERPULSE by Tessa Richter

40 years exploring and teaching the benefits of music, meditative states of flow, artistic creation, mindfulness, meditation, and mindset techniques. Coaching professionals to find their voice, meaning and purpose, and to perform at top level. Coaching individuals and groups on how to deal with stressful situations and change, and reframe crises in a positive manner to create health, happiness and purpose, leading to more success in all areas of life.

Our
Secret
Potential

A new approach to purpose, performance
and well-being in the 21st century

Tessa I. Richter

First published by INNERPULSE
© 2020 Tessa I. Richter

The right of Tessa I. Richter to be identified as author of this Work
has been asserted by her in accordance with sections 77 and 78 of
the Copyright, Designs and Patents Act 1988

ISBN: 978-3-9525298-0-5

A CIP catalogue record for this book is available from the British
Library

Cover design by Mark Jackson

Typesetting: Fuzzy Flamingo
www.fuzzyflamingo.co.uk

*I dedicate this book to love and cooperation and the new world
they will help to create. One that we will like to be a part of
and proud to have contributed to.*

Contents

WANT TO CREATE A
WHOLE NEW LIFE?

n my life, in spite of – or perhaps because of – great challenges, I have performed what I can only call miracles. Things I never ever in my wildest dreams would have deemed possible. I have also healed myself from major and minor illnesses, finding my own approach along the way.

As a teacher and coach, I have witnessed countless miracles. I'm not talking about the kind of miracle where you feed thousands with one piece of bread. But personal miracles we don't believe to be possible, such as healing from an incurable illness or finding a satisfying and well-paying job at the age of 60.

We consider them to be miracles, because they don't occur in a linear fashion as cause and effect. There are other principles and forces involved, such as quantum leaps, faith, listening to our inner wisdom and cooperating with life, based on trust.

It is this new approach to life, to the world we live in that I'm introducing here. May it serve as the basis for many to heal and create miracles, to perform at a whole new level. Moving into these possibilities is like moving into a whole new world, so very different from the world we live in. It is a world of cooperation, connection, and undreamt of possibilities. Once you've experienced it, you will never want to go back. You will be changed forever, and you will help change our world.

OUR LIFE CALLING

It is often our own life that reaches out to us, calling us and asking us to step into something completely new and unknown. Many times through an illness, losing work or a person, sometimes through an inner nagging, a feeling of: "I just cannot go on like this. Something needs to change."Collectively, we have begun to feel a deep unease. Mental illnesses, stress and burnout are causing our health insurances, companies and the state, enormous amounts of money.

Perhaps because of this, people all over the world have begun to look at our world in a different way. Looking for alternatives. We are beginning to realise that we have unused potential waiting to be unlocked. One that will bring an entirely new level of health, well-being and perhaps our own form of paradise.

30 years ago, I was ridiculed in my community for going round hugging trees. It kept me sane, when nothing else did. Things have changed. Today, scientists the world over are beginning to share their findings

that "forest bathing" in Japan or prescribing nature in Scotland are beneficial, and perhaps even vital, for our health. There are films showing evidence of the "intelligence of trees". And much more. We are not only moving into an era of unimaginable technological feats, but also into a new age of humanity. This movement is taking us both forward into the unknown, as well as backward, in that we are reconnecting to our deepest roots.

It is perhaps no coincidence that Japan, one of the countries known for its technologically driven culture, is at the forefront of this new movement. Technology and AI have become driving forces, better at many things than us humans. At the same time, doctors of the NHS in Great Britain are prescribing art, music, meditation, dancing and nature against depression and stress-related illnesses. Arts teaching could become more important than math in the tech-based future, says a leading education expert at OECD. Perceiving humans as the most "perfect and highly advanced machine" the way we have done, no longer works.

In the age of AI and all it entails, it is time to radically rethink who we are and what we are capable of, so we can access hitherto unused potential. Intuition, inspiration, empathy and creativity are some of our core competencies which we have not learned to trust and utilise fully. Few of us have learned to listen to our own heartbeats or that of our lives.

Growing up, most of us learn to use the talents and

develop the skills that are in keeping with what our social environment thinks is best. At school, we fit in with the generally accepted values of our society and the times we live in. We develop an image of who we are, based on our background, skills and what we perceive to be good, right, acceptable or valuable. Rarely do we question the validity of collective beliefs. Usually we do so only if we have tried hard, given it our best and haven't been able to fulfil the demands put on us by others. Or, sometimes, when we get ill, either physically or mentally.

When we are sick, we usually treat the illness on a physical level with medication, therapy or surgery. We rarely think of our work, our attitude towards life or towards others and ourselves, as being a possible cause for illness.

Over the course of many years, I have come to realise that our well-being and ability to achieve our highest potential has another, hidden aspect: it is connected to us living our true nature as human beings, based on who we are. This potential is rather like a muscle: if we don't use it, it shrivels and its energy goes stale. This affects our mental and physical well-being, leading to anxiety, lack of energy and motivation, but also to more serious diseases.

Each one of us is a unique instrument of creation, defined by our background, perception and talents. When we use only those aspects that are acceptable to the norm and people around us, beginning with our families and schools, we deprive ourselves of great potential. Yet the energy from which we are cutting ourselves off can play a decisive role in creating what matters to us, including well-being.

To illustrate, let me tell you a story. A young man, around the age of 30, came to me for career coaching. His doctor had diagnosed burnout. He was off work regularly, generally lacking energy, and unable to breathe properly. Because he also wanted to change direction in his career but didn't know what he wanted to do and how to go about it, he was referred to me by a friend.

After our first coaching session he said he was able to breathe for the first time in ages. And after a year he had changed careers and was doing exactly what we had found out together he wanted to do. Just as he had hoped for, he was working within the same company, but in a team he loved with colleagues who really appreciated him.

What did we do that enabled this? The process was simple, though not always straightforward and easy. There were several crises along the way, times when we didn't know where this would lead. In the first session we created a space of acceptance and trust. The issues that had led to his burnout were openly acknowledged, addressed and taken seriously. This is what I call "loving who you are", one of the keys to accessing our full potential.

During the course of our next sessions, we went on to explore his strengths, his values and the kind of environment that helps him create success in his life.

This is the part of "knowing yourself", another one of the three keys to unlocking hidden potential. The process of getting to know ourselves, I may add, continues for as long as we live. New potential can be developed at any age. And once we've activated hitherto unknown strengths, there are new ones waiting to be discovered.

Let me expand on this idea. If I needed to care for a plant or a tree, I would first have to find out what kind of species it is and its needs in terms of water, light, soil etc. I would need to know the best environment to plant it in and where it can thrive and produce fruit. In turn, its fruit is capable of nourishing many people. If I plant it in the wrong soil, over-feed it or don't water it enough, it will ultimately die. We usually take good care of plants, why not do the same for ourselves?

Taking a next step to creating something that matters in our lives, is the third key to unfolding our hidden potential. In the case of my young client, we explored who he was and what he liked doing and, most importantly, focused on loving those aspects. We then found that in his work, up to that point, he had always liked coaching, teaching others and helping them to do a better job at selling. As a sales person he had also done some sales training. This led us to think about a career move from sales to training.

And this is where the fundamental principle to bring our potential into the world kicks in. I call it co-creating. We will be most successful, happy and healthy if we learn to co-operate with life as it is, rather than imposing our wishes, or ignoring what life is offering us. We need to start exactly where we are, with life as it is and under the existing conditions. It's no use waiting until everything is the way we think it should be. Conditions will never be right for us to do what we most want to do.

In the case of our young man, the most obvious next step was to look into further education for him to become a trainer, but we also remained open to other options. He activated his network inside the company and someone came up with the idea of doing a kind of "taster day" in the training department he wanted to work in. On that day, he did a really good job and met people he liked and who liked him. Unfortunately, they didn't have a job for him at the time.

The process of finding his next step was not linear. He continued looking for other options and applying for jobs in other companies, at the same time keeping his desire to work in that training department alive. And, despite all his doubts, crises and uncertainties, after a year he was exactly where he wanted to be. He had managed to change jobs and was now working in the training department of the same company. When I saw him, a few months later, he was very happy. And just as important: his health was restored and he was completely revitalised.

I had assumed that he would heal given the right environment and the right occupation. I also believed in his secret potential, which would push him to step outside his current comfort zone. Besides more traditional tools, we used music and meditation techniques to help him relax. Relaxing is a key element in opening up to new possibilities and to life in general. Otherwise, it's rather like trying to fill more water into a full glass: you need to empty it first. If it's full it will overflow.

We also used images to describe his inner vision and to gauge how far he was in implementing this vision. And last, but not least, I created the necessary space to allow him to believe in a major change of career and lifestyle, until he trusted himself, and life, to make this move. He wanted more than anything to change his life, but he was also very much afraid. This is true for many of us. We grow to feel secure in what we've built, even if it no longer makes sense. And sometimes to the point where we get sick.

Making changes in our approach to life, in what we do professionally, or in our attitude to ourselves, has a profound impact on us and on our health.

Life has a way of presenting us with many opportunities which we can miss if we focus too much on what we want, what we think is possible or necessary, or on how things should be. If we realise that life is here to support us and that it has endless highly creative ways of helping us get to where we want to go, we can see the opportunities that will take us to places we could never have dreamed of.

THE STUFF MIRACLES ARE MADE OF

The world we live in is changing at a fast pace and many traditional structures are disintegrating. If we wish to actively co-create in this new world, we will need unused or only partially utilised abilities. These include parts of ourselves that, so far, were relegated to our private lives or considered useless, because they are not controllable and measurable. But today bears the incredible chance to combine ancient wisdom and modern science. An increased understanding of the findings of modern science about our universe will help us understand how to best move forward and perhaps create our own miracles.

MODERN PHYSICS MEETS ANCIENT MYSTICS

More and more people, especially physicists, biologists, but also business men and women and those engaged in the cultural sector, are becoming interested in the findings of modern physics as a base for a different perspective on everyday life and the world we live in. The insights of quantum physics have been used widely for technical appliances such as computers and scanners. But for us "normal" people it is still rather difficult to transfer this knowledge into our lives, after having completely internalised Newton's view of the world as a place governed by linear physical laws. Linear denotes a relationship of cause and effect, one incident causing another. We find it hard to believe that our world may function quite differently.

The most fascinating theories of modern physics are the quantum theory, the Field-theory and the "morphogenetic fields" of Rupert Sheldrake. I also found interesting food for thought in the science of chaos, confirming some of the insights I gained when inspired by nature. Though not strictly scientific, I would also like to include the psychologist C.G. Jung with his concept of synchronicity, a phenomenon which I have observed time and again in my own life and that of my clients. It can be explained through modern physics.

In quantum physics it is said that a particle can exist both as a wave and a particle. If it is observed, the location is fixed and it then becomes a particle. Otherwise it exists in a kind of ambivalent, original state as a wave. By observing a wave it becomes "solid matter". Reality is thus directly linked to the observer and, literally, what I observe becomes my reality. We co-create reality at the very core of matter. Where my focus goes, is where my reality unfolds.

Subatomic particles are, moreover, capable of

communicating and cooperating with each other. They are so closely linked with each other that they communicate across great distances without loss of time. Spatial and temporal separations do not exist on this level: the information is in different places at the exact same time. This is called the phenomenon of simultaneousness. In my opinion this is the basis for what Jung calls synchronicity.

Jung's "synchronicity", as opposed to causality, is the application of the scientific insights of quantum theory to the human psyche. It was always assumed that events in our lives were connected through a causal chain, one event causing another. As in physics, so in psychology. Jung, however, observed that events can be connected in a synchronistic way, without one of them having caused the other. These incidents are often perceived as coincidences in everyday life: the phone rings just as we are thinking of someone, or we are concerned with a question and somebody, even without knowing it, gives us a hint or an answer. This also explains why inventions are made in different places, all over the world, at the same time.

Regarding life as a simple chain of cause and effect, of un-moveable facts and fixed objects has become obsolete. Everything is vibration and all is interconnected. Reality no longer exists detached from myself and my perception. So, if I change, this will also have an impact on my life and the very reality I live in.

Many indigenous people, amongst them the

Aborigines and the Native Americans, believe that rocks and mountains are alive and that animals and plants have a soul. They also believe that we create beings and elements of nature by naming them. The Genesis of our Bible states that in the beginning was the word and the word was God. Virtually, by naming something, perceiving and recognizing it, we create it. Might this be a parallel to the perception of a quantum particle?

Sheldrake, for his part, speaks of morphogenetic fields, in which each thought, every feeling and any event is stored. The more people do, or think the same, the bigger the corresponding field. He reckoned that proteins and genes can no better explain the physical shape of living beings than building material on a building site can explain the form of a house. Everything, from molecules and organisms to societies and galaxies, is determined, in his view, by morphic fields, connected by resonance with similar systems and fields, of all cultures and all times.

This implies, amongst other things, that the field of a thought becomes bigger the more people think that thought. I find this very comforting, for it means that I do not have to effectuate all innovations myself. It is enough for me to think a certain thought and thereby contribute to spreading it, until the field is so large that it is easy for many people to have this same thought by tapping into the field. It also explains how certain skills evolve and spread, more readily accessible to everyone. The bigger the field of a certain skill, the more people are capable of it, and the easier it is for anyone to develop that skill. It is also a good thought model for how we co-create the world we live in together with each other.

The Field theory takes this idea a step further, combining many different findings of science. It assumes that there is one Field that connects all there is. In this Field, all existing information is contained, and everything determines and influences everything else. Through this Field we have access to any information that exists in the present, the past and the future. This, of course, enhances the idea of each of us being co-responsible, a fact we are more and more becoming aware of through ecology and the worldwideweb. And now the spreading of a virus.

The idea of the Field could be where modern physics meets ancient spiritual traditions, and it might be what mystics such as Krishnamurti experience directly in their entrancement, when they say: "You are the world".

For me, the most revolutionary idea of the Field is that memory is not something inside of us, but that the brain is an instrument with which we can retrieve any information we need from the Field. So instead of "thinking" we would be "receiving". According to this theory, we would be in a kind of constant interaction with the Field, and this would also explain creativity and intuition.

Quantum physics and the Field theory offer a scientific explanation for the fact that we can perceive beyond our senses, a phenomenon called "extrasensory perception". In times of climate changes, viruses and terrorism, we could be paralyzed by fear and loss of control. An alternative would be to link up with other levels of consciousness, to tap into the information needed for our survival. This, in turn, can provide a feeling of security and of being protected. Communicating directly with The Field can help us find orientation, make the right decisions, and intuitively be in the right place at the right time.

How do we tap into this information? We can receive direct impulses from the Field in the form of thoughts, feelings, sudden inspiration and insights. Before looking into this, let us however learn a little bit more about the stuff our reality is made of.

MYSTERIOUS INNER PULSE

Just as music with its beautiful melodies, catchy rhythms and harmonies is held together by its inner pulse, so are we. It is what gives us our unique drive and purpose. This pulse is connected to the pulse of the world around us, to that of others and to that of life itself.

Modern science tells us that vibration, or pulsation, is the basis for our entire universe. Vibrations have frequencies and are a form of energy. Everything in our universe pulsates, vibrates: all beings, including plants, organic material, organs, cells and even matter which we think of as "dead". Each thing, being and phenomenon has a pulse, a vibration of its own, including colours, feelings and thoughts.

This is what I call the "mysterious inner pulse": it is at the very core of our being and of the universe we live in. This term conveys some of the awe and respect I feel towards life, as well as some of the magic that can create miracles.

These inner pulses of things are perceived as the spirit of things, situations, places or groups of people, and can also be easily understood with the theory of Sheldrake's morphogenetic fields. We can connect to these fields, gain information from them and even communicate with these "spirit-fields-pulses". I would caution you to only do this with an attitude of co-operation and love. Anything else, like wanting to control situations for your own personal benefit and power, will inevitably backfire. So, when you do this, bear in mind the good of all of those involved.

In former times, people believed in destiny, God, or spirits of nature, and believed that if they abided by certain rules, no harm would come to them; they would be healthy and have all they needed for their survival. In those days, people had someone to translate what these Goddesses or spirits wanted to tell them, wanted them to do or not do. There was a kind of messenger-translator who was more powerful, in that respect, than any other person, because they alone were able to connect directly. These were called shamans, priests or oracles.

Today, we can connect directly, without any

intermediary, to the universe, spirit or the mysterious inner pulse. We no longer need these connectors to do it for us. This gives us our power, and our place in the world. It also means we are accountable.

This path is a radically new approach to life. It cannot be explained in terms of dogma or rules, for it is one that is different for each one of us. It also implies a revolutionary approach to our bodies, to our health, and also to performing things that otherwise would not be possible. We are becoming aware of being co-creators of life. I truly believe this can solve many, if not most, of the problems we face today.

If everything has a pulse, what happens when they interact and connect? Resonance is one of the most interesting phenomena in this context for us. If you have two pendulums one beside the other and you activate one, then the other will begin to adapt its swinging movement and, ultimately, they will vibrate in "unison".

We are constantly receiving vibrations from our surroundings. Each vibration has a certain frequency, in other words wavelength and a certain strength or volume, i.e. width of the pendulum swing. The same frequencies overlap and reinforce each other. There is resonance.

Most of us have experienced this: we enter a room, we feel the atmosphere. If we are in sync, we feel at ease, at home. If we're vibrating at a different rate, we feel uneasy. Depending on the strength of our own feelings, we can influence that of the room or vice versa.

If we understand that there is The Field, where

everything is connected to everything else, we realise that it is possible to communicate with just about anything. We can tune in and resonate with, basically, any other pulse out there. How do we resonate with a stone, you may ask? Ancient shamans and healers had no problem with this. It is in our genetic heritage to do so. What has changed are our beliefs. We no longer believe this to be desirable, let alone possible. This is another example of how the lens through which I choose to look at reality will determine how I experience and create reality.

You do not need a specific technique, but there are certain things that favor an exchange with the universal Field. Going into those sacred spaces, in which external sensory stimuli or physical activity are reduced, favors a way of connecting inwardly. It is also vital to trust that it can really work. What will definitely support this form of communication is a strong desire to communicate, a personal motivation, with purpose and love being the strongest enabler. We can open up to this inner process that cannot be entirely controlled, as if we were trusting ourselves to the current of a river, not knowing where it will take us.

Feelings, situations, other people and places, all have an inner pulse that we can tune into. This can be very helpful in trying to get more and different information from what we know with our conscious minds, from what is apparent and obvious, or already known.

Let me add, that this is what good oracles do. They have the capacity to tune into these fields, into the vibes of a place, into the pulse of an event. Whereas oracles do this for counselling, shamans use this technique for healing. They connect with animals and plant spirits or totems.

You and I can also do this. It takes openness, receptivity and practice, like any skill. And you will need to be familiar with different states of consciousness. In a very active mode, it will be difficult to receive accurate information. Rather like a full glass that has no room for more. So being able to go into alpha or even deeper states of relaxation to clear your mind is a first step. Love will be the best guide into the unknown, making sure you don't harm yourself or anyone else in the process, and the intention of what you wish to achieve, i.e. healing, will lead you to the answer. This will be perceived as inner wisdom.

Looking outside rather than inside, connecting our own inner pulse with the universal pulse outside of us, we can receive clues through synchronistic events or signs that life gives us, often through other people. When, several times in a row, something is said about the same idea, event, person or situation, it may well be worth listening to. Perhaps some greater intelligence is trying to get your attention.

LOOPHOLES OF CREATIVITY

Looking at the world through the lens of the theory of Chaos can add another insight into how we co-create. We all know and we've all experienced that life does not stick to our plans. Yet most of us are still brought up to believe that we can control what happens in our lives and that if something goes wrong it is our fault, believing that we did not try hard enough, or took the wrong decision, causing the current disaster or ill fate. What if we just don't have that power? What if there is an element of chaos, of unpredictability in any creative life-process? What if mistakes are life's way of showing us another possibility?

Did you know that a healthy heart has a slightly irregular beat? I saw this depicted in a book about the science of chaos. The representation of a perfectly regular heartbeat is that of a patient who died a few days later, whereas the picture with some deviations is that of a healthy heart. I was convinced it must be the other way around. In other words, nothing in nature is ever as precise as a machine or a computer. The small gaps of irregularity account for our lives, they account for us being alive.

The science of chaos offers clues as to how we can co-create our lives in these small gaps and loopholes. It demonstrates that we can use a subtle form of power, greater than any external power such as money and political power. This is illustrated in what is probably the best-known image of the science of chaos: that of the butterfly. The batting of a wing of a butterfly at one end of the world can influence the weather at the other end of the world and can even cause a hurricane. The tiniest incident can have a huge impact. Just like this butterfly, we have the power of subtle, but effective influence.

When we set out on a project, most of us have an idea of what we'd like to create. And we get upset if we don't achieve the desired result. We believe that a great artist knows what he or she's doing, can reproduce certain results infinitely and will produce exactly what he or she sets out to do. While technique is an important tool for creation and one that needs continuous refining through practice, it is but one aspect of creating. I've found that real satisfaction and fulfillment come from giving my all in terms of energy, technical skills etc, and then allowing the unintentional to enter and play its part in the process of any type of creation.

To become a channel for creation you need to be able to step out of the way and allow this unintentional creative force to enter into the creative process. Many great artists and composers call this creative process God. I would call it spirit or universal energy. Allowing spirit or universal intelligence to co-create, makes for surprises and creations we could never have dreamt of in our wildest dreams, in art, in business and in life. Creating and performing this way is a profoundly spiritual experience because it makes us feel part of something greater, something that goes way beyond just me. It connects me to the creative source of life itself.

Illustrating this point is the picture below. I was filming my statue of Sarasvati "the goddess of rivers, art, music and wisdom" when suddenly I saw another goddess appear in the river in the stone next to her on the right. It was one of those moments that connected me to the mysterious inner pulse of life. Never could I have planned for this.

Sarasvati on the left and the appearance of a
water goddess on the right

The process of co-creation, of allowing the unintentional or spirit to enter, can also be observed in healing. Here, it is often termed spontaneous healing or miracle. When doctors and scientists can't find a rational explanation, they have, in the past, chosen to ignore it. This aspect of healing is now beginning to receive some attention.

I am glad that life will always offer us unplanned experiences. I believe that unforeseeable experiences carry a great treasure which a large part of our culture draws from in art and music. This is the place where free will, inspiration, evolution and creativity are located. It is also the "human or natural element" that sets us apart from the mechanical and technical. Just imagine the universe unfolding and evolving exactly as man or a machine conceived it. What a nightmare!

Let us then assume that life is on our side. That these loopholes of creativity are places where universal intelligence enters into the game. And that this greater force actually wants us to succeed, to be happy and healthy, to create what really matters in our lives for ourselves and those around us.

I have come to realise that believing this will give my life so much more meaning, and myself so much more power in dealing with hardship and unexpected challenges. It makes everything worthwhile. I truly believe that life is our partner, wanting only the very best for us. This is because life is so much greater than us, and universal intelligence can come up with so many unbelievable paths to where we want to go, unimaginable even in our wildest dreams.

This is also true for daily life. Yesterday, on a Sunday, I was craving some peace and quiet. And I was feeling fed up and overwhelmed with noise. Noise from my neighbours, from planes flying overhead at a rate of one per minute, noise from the tennis courts opposite my house. I tuned into universal energy, willing it to show me a place where I can regularly go to get away from civilization. Well, tough luck. It did not bless me with an answer or idea. I was invited to a fare-well party, another painful event that day. So, I got in the car and was on my way when I suddenly realised I had passed the motorway exit I was supposed to take. This annoyed me, but I had no choice but to take another route. I decided to not drive back to my usual route, but instead I took another route through a little valley. This turned out to be one of my little blessings of the day. It was green and lush, and, as I was driving through it, my heart opened and I felt a moment of temporary peace come over me.

At the party I was blessed again in an unexpeceted an unplannable way. One of my best friends was moving to another country. She introduced me to her other friends and I ended up talking to another writer with whom things immediately clicked. We had several topics in common and what sealed our new connection, making us want to meet up again, was the fact she has the same name as my mother's maiden name, also of Scottish descent. This was, indeed, a huge present from the universe, giving me a chance to see beyond my friend leaving me.

I find that ready-made concepts are out-of-touch with life and actually impede it. I believe we will have the highest level of energy at our disposal if we act in accordance with who we truly are, and if we connect with some kind of universal source, the well-being of all in mind. Having a personal vision and being able to hear our inner voice will best lead us into the future. What gives us strength is trusting in things being right just the way they are – even if we may not perceive them as such – and based on this assumption, finding our own creative solutions. Every human being is, in part, responsible for his or her life which does not mean that we can control it. It means we decide where to focus, and where we chose to help life unfold.

As everything we are, and everything around us, is a form of energy with which we can resonate and communicate, I feel that ethics and aesthetics cannot be separated, meaning that healthy ethics cannot develop in a cold, unnatural, colourless and lifeless space. Take a look at most of the places where business is done. How would it be if we conducted business outside, in nature or in colourful, organic surroundings?

All aspects of life are part of nature, including mud, dirt and poisonous plants. Last but not least, there is no separation between body, mind and spirit. They are the same in different states, just as water, normally liquid, can also exist in the state of ice or steam.

OUR SECRET POTENTIAL

Each of us has a unique potential. No other person is exactly like you. Most of us have not uncovered all of our skills, talents and dormant abilities. This secret potential is made up of different aspects of ourselves that we have not yet fully acknowledged, expressed or developed. Some are skills we had as children, and we have lost or unlearned on our way to growing up. Others were simply never developed for a variety of reasons: lack of time, having to earn a living, our parents telling us what is right or wrong, society accepting only certain types of behaviour, to name but a few. We have learned to live with what is acceptable and feasible, not necessarily with who we truly are by nature.

There are two basic categories of unused potential which we will look at: that which is deeply personal, that which only you have, and that which our society has discarded and deemed unusable, unreliable, not relevant. For whatever reason.

A recent study carried out by NASA explored creativity in their staff, to evaluate their potential for jobs and development. The question arose: are we born with a certain creative potential? The result was astounding. By the standards they had set with grown-ups, 98% of all children aged four to five fell into the genius category of imagination. What is remarkable and interesting for us, is that they found this very high percentage drops rapidly as we grow up, and go through educational systems that focus on other skills. At the age of 30 a mere 2% of the people involved in the study were still creative geniuses. We all seem to unlearn this intrinsic skill as we grow up.

Luckily, we can re-activate this potential and tap into it, as it may be in hibernation and never entirely lost. Simple ways to do so, starting immediately, include day-dreaming and performing small creative activities, or simply doing things differently from the way we are used to.

Another, more individual, potential also goes back to when we were young. As youngsters, we often have dreams or wishes for our lives ahead. These can be as concrete as becoming a doctor or as vague as traveling a lot. Some dreams come true, others we incorporate into another life, i.e. you may not have become a professional writer, but you write wonderful love letters, or have become a prolific blogger in your spare time. And sometimes life has taken us completely down another road, but is suddenly knocking on our door to re-activate this dream that has been inactive for many years. Now could be the time to go back and remember what it was you dreamed of, what you really enjoyed doing as a youngster, up to the age of 14.

Besides creativity, there is another potential which contemporary Western society has relegated to the back seat. It has to do with artistic, musical, intuitive and inspirational skills. Our society has come to value the brain, particularly the part which analyses, plans, rationalises and is capable of technical feats, as the most precious asset for our society and a successful life.

But, as we are discovering, we also have two more brains, representing different forms of intelligence: the heart and the gut. We all know they exist, and that they have a tremendous power to guide us and lead us to where we want to go through our intuition, inspiration and a gut feeling. These are part of our inherent potential to help us create and live meaningful lives. Unfortunately, most of us have learned to distrust them, considering them as inferior to the rational mind. We are made to believe that these parts of ourselves have no value. Yet it is precisely the heart and the gut that can produce miracles and deep satisfaction. "Imagination is more important than knowledge", as Einstein said a century ago.

ACCESSING OUR SECRET GARDEN

Over the course of my life, creating works of art and new professional paths for myself, I have discovered that there is a triad, a spiral rotating in all directions, which enables us to open the hidden door to what we have inside of us, to that which is not yet expressed. This will help us recognise, nourish and grow the seeds of our potential, and bring them to blossom. It is: know yourself – love who you are – and create what matters.

You can be anywhere in this triad. To enable well-being and top performance, all three aspects are important, even if only one is active at the current moment. One will take you to the next. Rather like three keys that open the gateway to full fruition, one allows you to peek into the secret garden and all three get you inside.

If you're lacking just one of these three, you may well get sick, as I experienced a few years ago. In my case the missing link was loving myself. I had always followed my passion, first in music, becoming a professional musician, then as a visual artist, painting and sculpting. I was successful in both, having followed my inner calling. I had "known myself" and "created what mattered". And in spite of that, I had fallen seriously ill, which made me question my life up until then. At this new crossing in my life, using one of the techniques I had developed, which was to tap into my own inner wisdom, to connect to my inner pulse, I received the following answer: "You've learned to love others unconditionally, it is now time to learn to love yourself in the same way."

Once again it was an illness that triggered full potential. I developed my own way of loving myself, which we will explore later. By learning to love myself, I re-created a new cycle of getting to know another part of myself, and have since started to create an entirely new life, based on this new potential. I never knew I had it in me to be a "business person", capable of helping other business people and professionals to find their purpose and market themselves. I never thought I would understand a world that up to then had been totally foreign to me. And I certainly didn't believe I could be of help in accessing unused potential and help create what matters in the lives of so many. Though that is what I always wanted to do, deep down. This new potential and cycle of creating what matters to me, is prompting me to write this book.

Let us look at all three keys individually and perhaps you can begin to see where you're at, as well as which one could possibly unlock more of your secret potential.

KNOW YOURSELF

Most of us would probably contend that we know ourselves. We define ourselves through our background, upbringing, education, experience and the environment we live in. And we tend to see ourselves as a fixed product that is capable of certain things, using certain skills, and not capable of certain other things.

We don't always realise that our beliefs and ideas about ourselves are rather limited, remaining unaware of all our talents. It is important to understand that living to the full means changing perspective on who we are, stepping outside of our comfort zone and being daring. It is often in a situation of crisis that we are driven to do this.

More often than not, it is life that brings opportunities we could never have dreamed of. It is life that destroys our concepts of who we are, shows us limitations and re-directs us. That is why, in understanding how we create our lives, it is important to include life as our most important partner of creation. It is what I call co-creating with life as it is. We will talk more about this later.

If every one of us is like a unique instrument of creation, who or what is it that creates through us? Who "uses" our unique talents and skills to create what matters in this world? We will most likely have our own interpretation of this, calling it our soul, the universe, universal intelligence, god, the tao or simply life itself. In any case, I believe it is something that is greater than our individual self. This force needs every one of us to create here on Earth. Because only you can bring what you are into the world. No one else can.

To use the full range of the instrument that I am, I need to learn to "play" it. Only I can do that. Only I know who I am, what I need, what supports me and what I would like to create. I am the expert on me. We lose a lot of energy trying to be someone else. Why not relax and blossom according to our own inherent plan?

Knowing yourself allows you to create a life that corresponds to who you truly are, not what people expect of you, nor what you think you should be doing

– for whatever reasons. Knowing yourself means you can look out for yourself, your own goals, needs, ways of doing things and personal values. You will thus tap into your own wisdom and inner knowledge of what is right for you, and you only.

There is an essential part of you which was created way back when you came into the world. Rather like a seed before it has become a plant or a tree. This seed is not negotiable. It is our very essence.

As in the image of a tree: the seed of a fig tree will always grow into a fig tree and will never become an oak tree. No matter how much you, or others, treat it like an apple tree, it will always remain a fig tree. It will bear fruit, if nourished according to its specific needs, or die. So, if you're a fig tree, why not find out what this fig tree needs to thrive, and what the conditions are that make for a lot of yummy fruit? Giving yourself the right environment for who you truly are, and asking others to help you create it, will allow you to grow and harvest wonderful fruit. And these, in turn, will also feed others. By your very nature, you, the tree, will give your figs, year after year, to the world around you. Others can savour, appreciate and use them. That is what the fig tree has to offer.

Begin by finding out what kind of tree you are. This is an individual and never-ending process which is as unique as you are. Getting to know yourself will only stop when you leave this Earth. In the meantime, it will most certainly take you to unknown territories and places you cannot imagine right now.

As much as the journey is individual and there is no recipe that's valid for everyone, there is something universal about a person being authentic. We can feel this. Many of us are inspired by people who have "found themselves". We can sense when someone has gone into the deepest depths of their soul and has come back with new treasures.

Our journey may begin by imitating such a person until we reach a point where we realise that our path is elsewhere. We outgrow our teachers. A good teacher, like a parent, will hold a sacred space for us to experience who we are, and for us to grow, until we can go off on our own.

LOVE WHO YOU ARE

Many of us perceive ourselves as not being good enough by the standards and demands put on us from early childhood, and through our upbringing, conditioning and experiences in school and later at work. This drives us to wanting to achieve more and more. It also means that we are never good enough. By nature, we are not meant to be perfect by other people's standards. We are also not meant to be the best possible machines. This can cause many problems, first and foremost health issues such as anxiety and burnout, to name but the most typical ones. It also means we don't accomplish what we we are inherently capable of.

We have not learned to love who we are. But, what if we were meant to be exactly the way we are? What if there is an inherent perfection in who we are, much like a tree is perfect, even though it doesn't grow like a computerised perfect plan, but totally unpredictably? And what if the environment we are born into, with its specific set of demands and conditions, helps us develop our inherent skills and talents according to some greater plan? What if this is not random and we don't just happen to grow into who we are? What if these conditions help us blossom into the flower we are meant to be? Even what is not developed or supported could then be part of a greater plan, one that includes exploring new skills later on in life.

Recently, I heard an amazing story of a woman who lost her job and whose husband couldn't work because he was seriously ill. With the minimal pension she was getting from the state, she and her family were not able to survive. She went round every morning, early so no-one would see her, collecting empty bottles for a few pennies.

In this phase of utter despair, needing extra money, an unused part of her potential, was triggered. She remembered her love for writing stories when she was younger. There and then, she sat down and started to write erotic stories. Her husband thought she was crazy. Under a pseudonym, she published her first erotic novel and was totally surprised to find 1000 Euro on her account the next month, after publishing it online. She wasn't expecting anything like this. A few years on and she has now been able to buy herself and her family a nice house with the money earned through her writing.

We all love this kind of story, as it touches something deep inside of us. What is important to realise, is that the principle is true for everyone. The facts aren't. Not everyone wishing to write will have this kind of success. It is finding what is right for you in the context of your life.

As a classical musician I spent most of the first 40 years of my life striving for perfection. Practicing every single day, with very few breaks or holidays. Striving always to become technically perfect, I realised at one point that I performed much better if I worked with the premise that I was perfect the way I was. I discovered the perfection of the soul. When my soul was expressing itself, technical questions moved into the background and there was a fresh and natural kind of perfection, just like the tree growing according to its inherent nature.

I realised that there is a kind of natural beauty in each one of us. We have not learned to see it, or hear it, because our eyes and ears are trained to perceive what should be a certain way, by certain standards. We are trained to look at ourselves through the eyes of others, of society and its regulations and demands. This external perception has become so engrained into us that we have a hard time stepping out of it.

A blossoming flower is perfect the way it is. If we imitate it on a computer in a perfect pattern, the image leaves us cold, it does not reach our soul. As I experimented with the effect images have on us, I found natural and imperfect images that have a "human and natural touch" to be far more powerful than anything generated by a machine.

The same is true for our body and its inner pulse. As we saw earlier with the theory of chaos and the irregular heartbeat: just as nature is not unflawed, we aren't either. A kind of perfect imperfection.

I am not advocating a laissez-faire that has no standards or ideals. Rather a kind of reaching for the stars with who you are, intrinsically, with your own personality, with your talents and your view of the world. And understanding that giving all you can, what you have, is enough. It need not be more.

We do not need to be better than others to thrive. Thanks to our uniqueness, the person next to me is as perfect as I am. I cannot be her and he cannot be me. This can be the basis for a new approach to living, one based on cooperation rather than competition.

It was not until I started trying to love myself that I realised how difficult it was. This, in spite of the fact, that by other people's standards I was doing what I loved doing: composing and painting. I realised that, deep down, I felt unloved and unappreciated. Mostly because many people simply didn't understand what I was about, what I was expressing in my life, my art and my music. I could see the beauty, but put myself down because I couldn't make others see it. I thought it was "my fault", my shortcoming and that I was to blame.

As I got sick and discovered the wisdom of loving myself unconditionally, I now had the huge task of changing the lens through which I had been looking at myself and my life. The new lens would be love. One thing I realised was that, if I don't love myself and appreciate myself, how can others do so? Or if they do, will I even be able to notice it, and feel it?

Loving who you are is a matter of choice. And you might as well choose to start now, because you're not going to change who you are in essence, no matter how much you may try. This decision will empower you to use all of your potential, including the part which you have kept hidden and those parts of you that you thought were unacceptable or out of reach or that you condemned, for whatever reason.

Loving who we are is creating space. It takes away the pressure, it allows us to connect with the highest version of ourselves. Pressure and fear are the forces that separate and divide. They are absolutely valid and part of our personality and our experience in a physical body. However, we can always decide to change perspective and choose love over fear. Love connects us to something greater: to others, to universal energy. Connected, we are so much more powerful than seperated.

The other day, speaking to a friend of how I've been practicing loving myself on a daily basis for the past years, she asked me: are you already there, or still working at it? Well, I said, it's an ongoing process and just as life never stands still, there are always new challenges to loving myself. Just as there are always new aspects of myself to be uncovered and expressed. This never stops for as long as we live.

Paradoxically, loving what exists creates the space for change. It's rather like being on a hike, checking and acknowledging your coordinates to see where you are at that moment. This allows you to proceed to where you want to go. If you don't know where you are, you cannot make a plan to get to where you want to be.

Loving who you are is the energy behind giving yourself what you need and asking others to help you create the right environment for who you truly are. Whatever you come into this life with, the seed you are at birth will want to blossom at some point in this life. If there remains some hidden part that has not yet grown into what it is meant to be, this part will knock on your door. We need to learn to listen to this gentle nudge of our inner voice. We have become adept at pushing it away, ignoring it, shoving it back to where it came from. Then life takes a turn for the unexpected: we lose our job, we get sick, someone leaves us. This is actually life cooperating with us, on its deepest level, giving us the chance to take another, deeper look inside ourselves. It is enabling us to step out of our daily routine and reflect and explore who we are. In this space we will be able to hear the inner pulse of our life knocking on our secret door. And because things aren't going so well, we're more likely to open the door and welcome what we find.

Loving who we are is perhaps the greatest key to accessing our full potential. It is the fuel that will keep you going when faced with obstacles, fear or criticism. Loving who we are could be the single most revolutionary act to change our world, practicing it on a daily basis the most challenging, and not giving up when faced with rejection or doubt the most sustainable.

CREATE WHAT MATTERS

Creativity is a form of energy, a force of nature. As such it is part of the human condition, of who we are intrinsically: we create new cells in our bodies every single day of our lives. On a less physical level, creativity is an energy we can connect with, like love. If knowing ourselves is finding out how we are wired, loving ourselves is switching on the current. And creating what matters is using that current to turn on a light, to warm up a house or mow the lawn.

In itself, creativity is neither positive nor negative. It is pure energy and it is up to us to channel it. Knowing myself and loving who I am is the focus, the channel through which I can direct this powerful energy. Creativity unchanneled can go stale and create havoc. We can create "healthy" cells in our bodies or „sick" ones.

If each one of us is a unique instrument of creation, only I can go about creating what really matters to me.

I will experience this as meaning and purpose. Purpose is more than passion. Whereas many people seek to live their passions, finding meaning is even more powerful. It takes us beyond ourselves and connects us with the world around us, giving our lives meaning. Living my passion is one aspect of who I am. Expressing meaning and purpose combines my skills with what is needed in the world around me. In the example above it could be providing light or warmth in my unique way.

What is it that you and only you can bring into the world? What is your particular song and how does it sound? What is it that you'd like to contribute to this world at the present time? It is time to think about how to express your unique you and take the first step in creating what matters to you.

CO-CREATING WITH THE
WORLD WE LIVE IN

Perhaps the 2020 world crisis, brought about through COVID-19, is all about creating what matters in connection with others.

Growing up I was led to believe that, as long as I worked hard enough, I could achieve anything. It was the American dream and German work ethic. Perhaps in my case it was also being into classical music, where practicing daily was essential, it was part of the deal. As a professional musician I practiced every day for about 30 years and thought this was the key to success.

Nobody talked to me about inspiration and allowing something greater to come into music, or into my career and my life. I started to explore this on my own through various techniques, such as trance and meditation, experimenting with how to become the instrument through which the universe can play music. When I started to paint and explored my creativity in a new way as a visual artist, I realised that there was again, induced by meditative music, something greater than me to tap into. I could allow this energy to flow into the painting without judging and without controlling it, just directing it. If I was able to let it be part of the creative process, I would feel more whole and more fulfilled. And happier with the result. When I finally got into sculpting, I extended this to co-operating with the material I was working with, i.e. the stone. I entered into a kind of a dialogue with the material I was working on. We co-created the sculptures together, the stone with its colour, shape and consistency, and me.

Another great creative adventure was composing, where I took what I had learned into a new field. I "composed" by giving myself a structure of harmonies/melody and/or rhythm, and then improvised. I made room for that un-known element that I had come to realise was always part of any creative process: my "co-creating partner".

In the West, we grow up believing that if we know the rules, we can use them to achieve whatever it is we desire. All we need to do is try and work hard and long enough. In this concept of life, we are the sole and unique actors and all depends on us. We are a kind of super machine. But now we have reached the limits of this concept of feasibility. Not everything that can be done should be done or even needs to be done. What are the criteria and guidelines by which we can decide what to create? How do we find that balance between what we desire and what makes sense in the larger scheme of things?

We are extremely fixated on the result in anything we do. We always need goals, and feel we should be goal-orientated and achieve what we set out to do. We learn to avoid making "mistakes" at all cost. This, however, will not get us our best results, i.e. the best product, best experience, best process. I have found that, when creating, it is important to separate the process from the result. If we identify too strongly with the result we want to achieve, we will not be free to allow more energy, or other forms of intelligence to enter into the process.

Because this is not something we learn as we are grow up, you may ask: how can we allow the creative process to unfold, with the unexpected and unknown as an integral part of it? Basically and foremost, by changing perspective, by looking at the material we're working with, whether a stone, a group of people, as a partner we can, and should, trust. One who knows something we don't, who is able to do things we can't, or inspires us to unfold other parts of our potential we were not aware of up to that moment. Enjoying the process itself is so much more rewarding and satisfying and will help us step out of the way for the co-operating element to be present. We become a kind of instrument, a channel for the creative force and universal intelligence. This greater force, life, creativity, some call it God, can flow through us, allowing us to use our abilities, our lens of perception and all of who we are, to create something unique.

In everything we create, there is an element of novelty, of entering new territory. Allow for this. An open attitude of experimenting can be conducive, rather than "knowing it all".

Successful people know that it takes practice, practice, practice and faith and trust in the process. When we don't get the desired result, we can either give up or we can keep going, remaining open to this process that will take us to unknown territory. It will transport us to a place we have never envisioned and known before. This can be one of the most challenging aspects of co-creating.

Let's begin to see ourselves as one part of the creative process, not the sole creator, rather a partner to other creative forces in our lives such as time, circumstances, life, people and resources. The unknown elements will always enter the creative process, whether we are creating a piece of art, a new business, good health or another life for ourselves.

We can actively invite this universal form of intelligence. I believe that the prayer "thy will be done" is a recognition of this, translated into Christian religious practice. At other times this universal partner will impose itself, through an outside event, mishap or unexpected present or offer. Look at the huge crisis we are facing in 2020. WE did not ask for this. Yet nature, life, universal intelligence is opening up a new path for us to try. It is up to us to see it as a positive force and channel it into the direction we desire for us as individuals and for our world.

Whereas in the old days things were done by "God's" will or that of the spirits etc., the last centuries have been about "my will shall be done". Perhaps the time has come when it is our joint will: something greater than me, working its way into the world through me, rather like through an instrument or a lens. I am of equal importance in this process because of who I am. Only I can create what I create, because there is only one of me.

It is essential to learn to hear what life is telling us through many different channels: our inner channels are intuition, impulses and inspiration and the outer ones synchronicity, signs and events in our lives. Co-creating with life takes place now, it means connecting with life as it is, exploring existing options that are present in our lives, but perhaps not visible at first sight.

LIFE HELPS US MOBILISE HIDDEN TALENTS

I recently met a woman who's been an artist all her life. I believe she struggled, like many of us, with making ends meet, but finally got a job that enabled her to live well, working as a trend researcher and designer for architects, a job she was very happy with and loved doing. When she lost it, it was a great shock. At over 60 years of age, it was also a real problem. A friend in Poland invited her to go and stay, to relax, regroup and reflect on her situation. While there, she got a chance to visit the University for Design in Krakow. Unexpectedly, they encouraged her to send in her CV, and she got a job as a lecturer.

Up to that point in time, this would have been the very last thing on her list of options as a means of earning money. She has had a stammer all her life and never thought she would be able to talk in front of an audience. Understandably, she was extremely nervous before her first lecture, where she was to address 250 people. And then, as soon as she started, a miracle occurred: she spoke fluently, with absolutely no stammer.

What happened? I believe she has a message for the world, or at least for those who want to hear it. The minute people were willing to listen to her, wanting to hear what she had to say, her full potential kicked in, and she was able to overcome any obstacles that had been holding her back. She got the job and loves it. For the first time in her life she feels appreciated for who she is. She finally has the chance to be that person. She was willing to go beyond everything she had known up to then, even make a fool of herself, and feel very uncomfortable, because a part of her knew there was a significant something to be gained.

Life was actually on her side, even though it may not have seemed that way. Had she not lost her job, she may never have known nor experienced this deep fulfillment. An interesting detail: years before this, even though she never thought of herself as a lecturer, she spent hours every day researching design trends and reading articles. This was to the point where the librarian asked her if she was a lecturer preparing her lectures. You could say that she, unknowingly, set an intention and acted on it.

This story shows us that there is absolutely no age limit to finding another part of our secret potential and living it. I believe life unfolds to help us see and express more and more, as we go along. Sometimes we can do it easily, following an inner call. At other times we are pushed forward by life itself.

WEAKNESSES: OUR GUIDES TO CREATING WHAT MATTERS

There are aspects of ourselves that are less accepted and which we commonly want to hide. By doing so, we are prevented from using our full potential. Uncovering these aspects and turning "weaknesses" into strengths is empowering, and opens up a whole new dimension to our lives.

I learned this when I helped one of my clients find his perfect job. This was a person who had come to Switzerland as an immigrant and was sensitive to feeling excluded. He developed a compensating behaviour for not belonging, which I believe became one of his strengths: an incredible ability to oversee the most complex situations, seeing both grand scheme and all the details. When working on a project in his job as an IT engineer and team leader, he astounded people by remembering things others would forget. However, this also made him rather unpopular, as people don't like to be reminded of their shortcomings. His company paid for him to be coached internally for nine months, in an attempt to "develop his social skills" to a level deemed acceptable by their standards. At the end of this period he lost his job.

When we started working together, we discussed his strengths and weaknesses and did an analysis of his potential. One of his greatest desires in a workplace was to be friends with his team members. His behaviour up until then had made this impossible. Rather than try to change him, I suggested he was perfectly alright the way he was, it was just the environment that wasn't suited to him. I suggested we find an environment where his high brain power was an asset and not something people loathed. This led to a simple solution: if he became an auditor, he would be using his strength in a positive manner, it would even be a key skill necessary to the job. At the same time, it wouldn't affect the relationship within his team, as everyone in his team would be going out on audits like himself, and they would all remain a team. After knowing what it was he wanted, he found a job immediately. Many months later he thanked me for making this change and he was still happy in his new position.

Is there something you have always considered a weakness that you think you might turn into an asset?

COOPERATING WITH LIFE AS IT IS

When you accept yourself as you are, and life the way it is, you begin to cooperate with the universe. This is your best starting point for whatever you're trying to create: supportive relationships, finding a meaningful job or good health. Co-creating can be planned to some extent. Yet there is a whole aspect that is unpredictable. This is why I don't believe in visualizing all the details unless you're 100% sure you know exactly what it is you want and what it should look like. I would recommend, when visualizing, that you imagine the feeling of the outcome, such as a congratulatory handshake or the applause of the audience, not necessarily the details of how to get there.

Let me illustrate once again with music. When teaching beginners to play the flute, what often happened was that they tried so hard to produce a sound – for unlike with a piano or a guitar you have to produce the sound through the way you purse your lips, blowing against the edge of the flute at a certain angle – that they were unable to play a piece in time with the correct rhythm.

I developed a technique where I had my students feel the inner pulse of the music, like a heartbeat that beats on and on, one they could feel inside themselves regardless of what they were playing. Learning to focus on that, rather than the sound they were producing, made them stay in that musical flow, in the energy of the entire phrase. It is rather like thinking in whole sentences as opposed to individual words. Once they stopped focusing on the sound, and instead concentrated on the beat, they actually produced a decent sound and played in time.

An interesting paradox that can be applied to life. We can learn to focus on the larger pulse, on the essence, and let the details take care of themselves in the process. The intention of the mind, the focus on the pulse, allows the rest to unfold. Focusing on the inner pulse of the music is like focusing on the intention. Much later in my life, reading about quantum physics and that energy follows the focus, I learned the theoretical backup for this practical experience I had had. It's as if the big wave of intention carries the small waves of coordinating sound and rhythm. Meaning structures the sentence, not individual words.

If my intention is strong enough, the details will follow. Let me give an example. I knew when exploring options of composing that I needed a keyboard. After trying out many different ones, I settled on a particular model. At that time, however, I didn't have the money to buy it, so I let it go until a year later when my partner bought it for me. You will read more about this later. The clear intention was there and the universe followed.

TIMING, RHYTHMS AND CYCLES

Timing is a key factor in co-creating life. If something just won't move forward or isn't happening, there may well be a reason for this. It may not be the right time, an element in your plan may be missing, or a skill not yet mastered. Synchronizing your individual pulse to the greater pulse is crucial in achieving your goals and leading a happy life. It is vital to well-being and performing with ease. And, ultimately this is one of the key factors for enabling miracles to happen in your life. Because we don't create miracles alone. We need life and the pulse of the universe to cooperate. This will take everything onto that entirely new level, away from linear thinking: our quantum leap.

Every moment in time has a certain quality. In the Bible, Ecclesiastes 3, there is a well-known text, which describes how for every enterprise and each event there is a right time: birth and death, losing and finding, even for loving and hating, war and peace, just like wailing and dancing. It is also written there that we, as individuals, can only do so much. God, universal intelligence, or life will do the rest, with everybody's interest in mind. It is actually describing our inner pulse and the greater pulse of life and the universe – termed God in the Bible.

In my own life, time always seems to play an important role. Much of what I wanted, wished for and planned, did not work out and materialise at once. Being at odds with this cost me a lot of energy, but seems to be a necessary process in being able to let go. Timing is decisive for substantiating any idea. Many creative endeavors fail because we don't understand this element of time.

Besides the right, or should I say, the fitting moment for an event, there are general cycles and rhythms. There is the rhythm of day and night, the yearly cycle, seasons, the duration of a life and many more. After inhaling, we need to exhale. In nature, active phases are followed by periods of rest. I find this especially impressive with hibernating bears. But plants also wither, die in the autumn, and sprout in the spring. They are seemingly dead, but continue to live underground, dozing and gathering new strength in the dark womb of the earth.

Rhythms go from out to in, active to passive, up and down and back again. Our achievement-orientated society has lost its understanding of this. Many people have lost the connection to these rhythms and also to the greater cycles of life. The spiritual, the higher, the universal is overruled by the earthly, practical, material and egocentric. Our overly active society always wants more, we are pushed to work harder, longer hours, forgetting there is another, equally important phase to any endeavour. Waiting, being passive and receptive, is essential for our survival because it connects us with something greater and meaningful. What's more, it allows us to listen to that universal pulse and synchronise my own to that of the situation I'm in. I believe that these states are necessary antipoles to our busy lives. They have something to do with the female aspect of our human existence. You could also call it an aspect of nature in a technological world. Once again, if we don't listen to these cycles, we may well be forced to become passive by something happening in our lives, such as losing our job, a miscarriage, a virus.

In my own life I try to recognise rhythms and cycles, even if I have to admit that periods of darkness and unclarity are hard to bear and accept. Understanding them as a natural and inherent part of the process, like a seed germinating, takes away a lot of the unnecessary suffering and self-blaming.

USING ALL OUR BRAINS

Getting to know ourselves unlocks the door to our hidden potential. Whilst there are many ways of getting to know who we are: tests, counselling and trainings, let us look here at aspects that are not generally talked about, mostly because not quantifiable and considered as untrustworthy and unreliable. They are some of the most powerful gateways to our deepest energy, connecting us to our inner pulse.

DIFFERENT PARTS OF THE BRAIN

In our brains there are remnants of our evolution as human beings. Without going into the technical details, suffice it to say that the oldest parts are geared towards survival: fight and flight mode. If we act on this information and energy, we are in a mode of fear, functioning instinctively and with only part of our brain active. While this is vital for our survival in some situations, we usually don't need it in the Western world for our everyday life. Yet, we have not unlearned to use this part. It kicks in all too often when not necessary, in a way that doesn't really help. In the past, it was vital to be able to mobilise all our physical strength in a critical situation, to run or fight. Today, we need coherence of thought and emotions to react adequately. This is a new skill we can and need to learn if we want to take ourselves individually, as well as the human species collectively, to the next level of evolution. One that enables us to heal and perform miracles.

The prefrontal cortex is the latest acquisition in the evolution of mankind, and responsible for such things as the alphabet, music, science and creative thinking. According to Villoldo and Perlmutter ("Power up your brain. The neuroscience of enlightenment") this is our future and it is all about love.

The good news for us is that our neuronal networks, the connections in our brains, are not fixed and can be changed and remodeled at any given time in our lives. By choosing, each minute of our lives, between acting out of fear and fighting/fleeing, or acting out of love, and cooperating, we actively and consciously create new paths and connections in our brains.

Whilst we don't have the choice of what happens to us, we do have a momentous choice as to how we deal with these occurrences. This is perhaps the one most important thing to realise as we move towards bringing all of what is inside of us into the world. We rewire our brains by the choices we make every moment of our lives. Science has shown that this can not only change our brains, but influence our genome for generations to come.

Taking this one step further, by choosing love – and we will look into what we mean by this in more detail – we create a certain morphogenetic Field according to Sheldrake, one which enables others to also access this wiring more easily, as it picks up momentum through the practice of many. It is interesting to note that the idea of loving ourselves has become quite popular. So, this is something already growing in our consciousness, in the Field.

Think of fear and love as two paths, one goes right, one goes left. One, fear, is a trodden path, one we've gone down a million times, which we have been taught to do by observing our parents and teachers, by society in general and generations before us. Then there is that new path, virgin territory and more difficult to find, harder to follow. It is easier to walk down a path that has been made and used by many, where we needn't think, than to step out into some overgrown territory, where we have to cut out our own path.

There may well be situations when, for our physical or emotional survival, we need to act instinctively and fight or run. It is a question of realizing when best to use which parts of our brain and how to connect them to work together in synch.

Most of us are probably still more centered in the lymbic part of our brains: we perceive people, situations and the behaviour of others as a threat. Others, those we call religious or esoteric, have chosen a path to enlightenment, and may be more centered in the frontal cortex. They know all about quantum physics, meditation and other spiritual aspects of life, but not what is going on around them, the day to day business. That alone, however, will not guarantee what we need to survive on a physical level. Neither will be using their full potential. We need both.

Besides the front and back parts of the brain, we also have the right and the left hemisphere. Our memory is situated in the right part of the brain. This is where raw information, data, images, numbers and facts are stored, in fact any sensation without exception. However, we only have access to the important data and sensations, and we only exploit about one percent of this databank, our memory.

The front left half of the brain is the logical-analytical one. It controls the right side, filtering the raw material out of the unconscious, only allowing relevant information into the conscious realm of the brain. This prevents overstraining and allows us to function in everyday life.

The right side is the creative part of the brain, which we activate by engaging in painting, music, dancing and other creative activities. Images also generally activate all the information stored in our brains. In gaining access to the stored data, we can obtain information about a situation which by far exceeds that of the conscious mind. This is very useful when we are confronted with having to make a decision or finding creative solutions.

Images can serve as guides in difficult situations and both images and music can activate sources of energy that are not accessible through words alone.

We also access the data stored in our memory through relaxing. Outstanding inventions happen this way. After having dealt in depth with all the data, facts, in other words all the necessary information that is now stored in the brain, the moment of Eureka happens when we go for a walk, do the dishes, lie in bed, or are under the shower. It happens in a state of relaxation, when we are no longer focusing on the problem consciously.

To activate all of these parts of the brain, and allow them to cooperate, let us look at how we can connect them. Later, we will explore many tools in more detail. Here, I would like to point out what you can start doing immediately.

When listening to certain types of music, and especially when playing music ourselves, there is literally a firework that goes off in our brains, visible in scans. The same is true for when we are at a physical peak, doing sports. When performing at the highest level physically and emotionally, all of our brain is involved.

Love also coordinates all the parts of our brain. In a brain scan, scientists saw how love connects all the parts of our brain: back and front, right and left. We need to understand that love in this context is not romantic and gushy love, but the more embracing love which the Greeks called agape. It is indeed one of the most powerful tools we have to access our full potential.

And I will venture one big step further than scientific findings: when loving, we not only connect all the parts of our own brain, we also connect with our bodies, including every cell, as well as our "other brains", which we will look at now. Through love, and this is what mystics of all ages talk about, we access the universe. This is where we become one. In modern terms, we connect to the Field. Please take a moment right now to ponder the implications. This is very powerful stuff!

OUR 3 BRAINS: HEAD, HEART AND GUT

We have 3 organs that enable us to access different forms of intelligence: the head, the heart and the gut. WE have not learned to differentiate them, use them consciously and coherently all together. This is actually one of our greatest unused potentials. The current supremacy of the head has put the other two in a position of neglect. They are perceived as inferior and not to be relied upon.

As Minouche Shafik, director of the London School of Economics said: "In the past, jobs were about muscles, now they are about brains, but in the future they will be about the heart."

Translated into our 3 brains: the past was about the gut and the physical body, the present is about the analytical mind and the head, and the future is about love, cooperation and using the heart.

In the West, we have come to value intellectual faculties far higher than manual skills. More and more, if you want to be successful in business, you need to go to university and study. In Switzerland people used to be satisfied with an in-depth apprenticeship, a hands-on combination of work and school, to become a carpenter for instance. Today, the appreciation and value of these professions and the way they are regarded has greatly diminished, which means they are losing their attraction and their standing.

In school and in our upbringing, we learn to use our heads to perfection, or I should say the analytical and planning part of our heads. We have forgotten, or are unaware of the fact, that we can access a huge part of our potential through our "other brains": both within our brain – left/right, front/back – and within our body: the heart and the gut.

Science is finding that these brains are at least as significant for high level performance and well-being as our "analytical brain". Whereas the head is the ruler, the planner, the one who sets goals and intentions, it also needs to control. We reason ourselves into certain types of behaviour or decisions, and push ourselves to perfection, even where not necessary or not useful. This is one of the typical behaviours that can lead to burnout.

The heart, on the other hand, finds meaning and sets priorities. It finds purpose and taps into a huge reservoir of energy that is not available to the head. It can make us grow beyond anything we could imagine. The heart knows no reason, it can love the impossible, the unacceptable. It is, as we now realise, the opener of the full potential of the brain: remember how love enables the brain to connect to the maximum?

Not the least of our brains, the gut, is our innate instinct, the call to action. I believe it is what we have in common with animals. It can make us react, move, interfere, when the head is still arguing or reflecting and the heart doesn't want to hurt or is caught in emotions. Many successful leaders claim to have followed their guts on their route to success.

To activate fully who we are, it is useful to look at our personal use of these three brains, as well as their current function in our lives. It is the interaction of the three, termed "coherence", that ultimately leads to a more fulfilled, richer and happier life, with purpose and well-being, enabling us to achieve more than we ever dreamed of.

We all know what it means if someone is incoherent due to pressure and anxiety: it is being unable to think "coherently". We can actively take steps to connect our brains and create coherence.

To better understand what we are doing when we use our different brains, let us look at where the information comes from that we are accessing. Where does knowledge come from? Is it stored in the brain? Or could it be rather like the modern cloud technology?

In the past, we believed that all our knowledge, our skills and the information we store, is physically in our brains. An entirely new approach, which I believe makes more sense, and is more in keeping with modern physics and scientific findings, is a challenge to our traditional way of thinking. It claims that the universal Field as described above, is a reservoir of knowledge, much like a cloud in technology, where everything is stored, from images, to ideas, feelings, plans and anything else we can come up with. And our brains are instruments with which we access this unlimited Field. Each brain then is a different type of instrument, its intelligence widely differing from the other two. Each has a different capacity to gain information, accessing different data.

Intelligence and creativity viewed in these terms, would be an interaction with the enormous databank of the Field, and inspiration the finding of the right information in it. Are we in constant contact with the Field and are insights, inventions and creations a result of a dialogue with the Field?

It is conceivable that with each part of our body we have a specific kind of perception and intelligence. Every organ is like a tinted lens through which we perceive things a certain way. Or, in this modern sense, a certain type of antenna with which to receive information or connect to the Field. Let us focus here on the head, the heart and the belly. We can learn to use each of them individually and in coherence.

Another new approach to intelligence, as opposed to the physically stored knowledge in specific parts of the brain, contends that intelligence has to do with connections in the brain: the more connections, the more intelligent we are. This finding is substantiated by medical research where people who have lost a part of their brain can regain those skills by developing new connections in their brains. This science is called neuroplasticity and has had the most miraculous findings. Unlike what we have been told, these new connections can grow at any age until we die.

And, if you think about it, creativity establishes new connections by combining things in a different way. Being creative is thus an act of intelligence! Communication can also be seen as a form of connecting. When invoking God, are we joining up with the infinite quantum Field of information? And could it be that clairvoyance or clairaudience are specific forms of intelligence, that people with these gifts have a different kind of perception with which they have a more comprehensive access to the Field? Do these people have more pronounced antennae or different "filters" than the majority of us? And are we able to learn from them?

If we are able to access all the data of the universe, this means we can get all the information that is important for us regarding a specific question or topic, and we can make decisions in an autonomous and responsible way. We are not controllable. It implies that a direct line to "God" or the Field is our birthright, and we do not need any middlemen like churches, other institutions, or psychics to tell us what is right and wrong for us.

Relying on our own perception furthermore implies

we can start trusting ourselves, our own view of the world and what is "right" or "wrong" for us. What this implies is that there is no one way to perceive the world, no one form of knowledge. What is important for me, may not be so for you. What is true for me, may not be true for you. Consider that you and I both look at a ball that's half red and half blue: if I look at the blue side, I will believe the entire ball to be blue. You, looking at the other, the red side, will perceive it to be entirely red. We are both right and we are both wrong!

HEAD INTELLIGENCE: INSIGHT

We all know that the head is good at analyzing, planning, "rationalizing". The head is our intellectual brain. It is currently the most highly valued of all forms of intelligence in the West. People with a high IQ are venerated. It is only recently that emotional intelligence has begun to be of interest and has become a new focus as we come to realise that our mental capacities are limited in dealing with many aspects of modern life and its challenges.

The fact that our heads are currently considered more valuable than the heart, is reflected in our language. We talk about the head of a company, not the heart. Interestingly enough, the heart would be considered important for the internal functioning, but inferior, and would probably, in most cases, be associated with a woman.

We all know it's time for a major change and this could involve the mind being part of something greater, rather than the sole dictator.

Having said this, the mind, of course, is an integral part of anything we want to do or achieve and has great value in planning, in understanding and structuring processes, making them manageable.

In any case, it is helpful to explore how it works and specifically how our own minds work, i.e. how we approach things. What are our individual and personal thoughts and beliefs on a topic? This is called the mindset.

A creator's mindset will be different from that of a bookkeeper. It has become common knowledge that the mindset can be decisive in whether we are successful or not. It influences how we feel about a situation. If I think it's wrong to ever fail and that, if I fail, that's the end of that venture, it will certainly affect everything I do and how I approach a project. If, however, I have learned that failing is an integral, normal and important part of creating something of importance, I will begin to explore my failure as a guide to activating some hidden skills or a new perspective.

Successful sports people use mindset techniques, involving visualizing and imagining, to achieve success. Why shouldn't we use these techniques too? I first started exploring mindset techniques, combined with meditation techniques in my musical career and found them to be really simple and effective for everyone. I now use them with business people to create new careers and businesses, as well as enable people to perform with more ease and in better health. They can help with anything you wish to create, from more self-confidence to better realtionships.

Affirmations can be useful in this context, but only if associated with feelings and images, as confirmed by an experience I had when coaching. A 57 year old client had been working in the banking industry for the past 20 years and desperately wanted to get out of that line of business. Needless to say, she was having trouble changing direction because of her age and experience. She was also caught up in a somewhat negative cycle of thoughts regarding her age, and as a result of having been let go for the second time in her career. When I asked her what her resources were regarding building mental strength, she told me about a friend who had given her some positive affirmations. The affirmations were fine, but somehow she couldn't feel them. She couldn't feel herself to be successful. We did a simple guided inner journey where I led her to an experience when in her life she had expereinced herself to be strong and successful. Then I guided her to let this feeling flow into the current situation. At the end of our coaching program, just after the last session, she got a job in her preferred region and work environment outside of banking, just as she had wished for.

In spite of the findings of modern physics, we still look at the world with a linear approach: if I do this, it will lead to that, an approach of cause and effect. Businesses make plans and budgets for certain periods and then things turn out differently. Yet business plans are considered the most important guarantee to the success of a startup. Since quantum physics, however, we have learned that there can be non-linear evolution which cannot be "explained" intellectually, like a jump, a total shift of paradigm.

So, how does the head fit into all of this? And when I talk of the head, I mean the left side, the analytical, the one we have learned to use most. It has its place as a gate keeper. New thoughts, insights and ways of thinking, leading to new paths of action and new feelings, should be run by this part of us. Rather like the parent of a teenager being the gatekeeper for safety: our "heads" make sure there is some sound evidence, some reasonable good sense that keeps us grounded. This will enable us to combine the old and the new. We need our heads, as we need our wits about us. There are situations where the head is invaluable.

Beyond this more practical aspect of using our heads, there is another one, one that can connect us to the inner pulse of life. It helps us access a higher form of wisdom through insight. Insights into a situation are extremely useful, motivating, and they help us embrace difficult situations. They can be vital for our good health in helping us reconcile facts and events in our lives that otherwise have the potential to break us.

Insights are an important way to connect to a higher

truth, something universal that is neither a feeling nor something to sense, but rather something to ponder. With ramifications. Insights can be ground-breaking, literally, by preparing the ground for new ways forward. They clear the way for something entirely new, never conceived before. They are gateways into new territories.

The insight that our 3 brains are a bit like radio transmitters picking up a certain frequency, not picked up by the other two, thus accessing different information in the Field, makes it clear that the most brilliant computer, which is like a super head-brain will never be able to do what we as humans can do. It doesn't have a heart and it doesn't have a gut. Therein lies our power for miracles and our true human potential. We need not fear competition from machines and computers, unless that is the only thing we aim to be.

HEART INTELLIGENCE: INTUITION

"Here is my secret. It is very simple: It is only with the heart that one can see rightly; what is essential is invisible to the eye." de Saint-Exupéry.

In the Lakota language there is an expression *cante ista* that means "the eye of the heart." It is, I believe, through the heart that we are interconnected with all of life. Through this lens of perception, there is no separate self. As Chief Seattle said, "Humankind has not woven the web of life. We are but one thread within it. Whatever we do to the web, we do to ourselves. All things are bound together. All things connect." It is the heart that enables us to feel, sense and truly understand this. When we're in love, boundaries disappear and we see things literally with different eyes. When we listen to our heart, this might be meant literally. Opening our hearts can mobilise so much of our potential. It can cause us to overcome barriers and to grow beyond our limitations.

There are different forms of love. Besides the love for a partner that includes passion and physical love, there is the love we feel for family members, friends, as well as that for a stranger. As a teacher of painting courses, I used to sit there after our guided meditation, while my clients were painting, and just feel pure love. It was a kind of all-encompassing feeling, not personal. It filled me up and created a space of acceptance for my clients to express. It was not something I sought out, it simply happened and I went along, bathing in this wonderful energy.

Besides love itself, there are also gratitude, forgiveness, appreciation, acceptance, to name a few. If you have trouble with the word love and what it entails, perhaps try one of these positive emotions that are other forms of love.

We have seen above that there are endless, chaotic fluctuations and variations in a healthy heartbeat, quite unlike any mechanical or electronically generated pulse. Our hearts are constantly beating to the rhythm of our feelings. In love we talk of our hearts pounding and two hearts beating in unison. A healthy heart is one that varies its beat according to the situation, one that adapts. It is flexible.

There is a mutual interdependence between heart and mind. A certain pulse has its corresponding psychological inner state: if I calm my heart, I calm my spirit and vice-versa. It is not possible to be excited with a calm pulse.

We all know how strong and overriding love is. Activating this force could literally be life-saving, for us on an individual level, but also collectively. Did you know that we can physically die of a broken heart?

The heart sends signals to the brain; heart and brain are always communicating. Our hearts influence what we think, how we think; they are an integral and vital part of our intelligence. Science has recently found that when we are in love, a certain part of the brain is very active. It is the same part that we activate when taking drugs, such as cocaine, meaning it is also our addiction center. So, while we think of love as being situated in the heart, it is also connected to the brain in our heads. Loving ourselves could actually be the solution to getting off drugs, to becoming independent of any form of addiction.

If we can activate that center with love for ourselves, we neither need drugs nor someone else to love us. Perhaps this is why many modern psychologists say: you need to love yourself first. I never really understood this. But, after practicing self-love for the past 5 years, I know it's true.

There is also a "higher" use of the heart for guidance, which is to tap into the reservoir of universal energy. We can use the heart to connect to our inner pulse through intuition. Intuition tells us something is right or wrong for us. Learning to trust our intuition is perhaps one of the great challenges we face, when wanting to express and live our full potential. Top performance is not usually associated with the heart. Athletes practice mindset and visualizing. Who talks about the heart?

When I was performing at the top level in music, no-one ever spoke about love and intuition. Perhaps this accounts for burnouts and anxiety with high achievers. It enhances stress, once you're performing at this level, in whatever field you're in, even if you're performing at your own personal top level. If we perform with love, we can access this extra energy: love for ourselves and love for those we are interacting with, as well as love for what we are doing. As a musician, if I convey love through my music, I can access a potent source of energy. This is not available if I perform simply out of wanting to achieve and succeed on a high technical level or wanting to be famous with lots of money.

If loving ourselves is one of the keys to unlocking our hidden potential, the heart is the instrument for this type of intelligence. It "knows" things that other parts of us don't. "le coeur a ses raisons que la raison ne connaît pas." It is time we understood that tapping into the heart's wisdom through empathy and intuition is perhaps one of the most powerful tools at our disposal to change our world. Don't allow fear and your "head" to get in the way. Otherwise, this channel of receiving information can get distorted and even dry up entirely.

GUT INTELLIGENCE: IMPULSE

Scientists have found our intestines, our enteric nervous system with bacteria and neurons, represent another, even more important brain than the one in our heads. A lot of information and sensations are stored here, mostly those that are not consciously accessible to us. Do we access this intelligence through instinct?

Some scientists actually speak of the gut as a "thinking organ" (Scheman). Head and gut also have the identical cell and molecular structure, so that medicine we use for our heads also works on the gut and vice-versa. Only recently, researchers found that more nerve cords go from the gut to the brain than the other way around. It appears that messages coming from the gut to the brain are more important than from the brain to the gut. When we take a decision, this is based on the unconscious stored emotions and body reactions. The wisdom of the gut exists, just like that of the heart.

Our gut is the largest organ of immunity, it is extremely powerful. Chi-Gong exercises aim to balance and strengthen the Chi. Seat of the Chi is the belly, the center of a person, according to Chinese philosophy. Breathing also originates in the belly, and in martial arts this is where our concentrated power comes from. Could "acting from our guts" mean mobilizing this energy? The belly is our physical center, the collective point of our energy and power. Instinct is what we have in common with animals. Animals access this "brain" with no barrier. It is responsible for both their, and our, survival.

Gut feelings are by their very nature irrational. You cannot argue with them. If you try to rationalise them, they will disappear. They don't have analytical and reasonable thoughts as their basis, but sub-conscious feelings and physiological reactions that are not accessible to the mind. Many successful business people will attest to trusting his or her gut feelings to having led them to succeed. Even if they have to rationalise and find arguments for a decision in order to convince other partners involved.

Premonitions are a special form of gut feeling. In an experiment, scientists recorded reactions to images a computer displayed at random: colour photos of relaxing scenes, such as nature or landscapes, or shocking and disturbing scenes, like autopsies or erotic pictures. As was to be expected, the bodies of the participants relaxed immediately when they watched peaceful scenes, and showed signs of agitation as soon as they saw erotic or repellent pictures. But what is significant in this context, is that the researchers discovered the test person actually sensed what they were about to see. They registered physiological reactions before the respective photo appeared on the screen. The reaction was strongest before a repulsive picture, as if the person were trying to guard against it.

If gut feelings are related to instinct and survival, it can indeed be life-saving to trust them and act on them, as I once experienced many years ago. I was waiting for a train and there were several platforms. One of them, the one next to the wall, also had what looked like an unused track on the same level as the platform next to it, i.e. not lowered down like all the other tracks. I was walking up and down this platform, lost in thought, until suddenly something urged me to step back, immediately, without delay! I responded, and shortly afterwards a train rushed past me on this track. I would not have stood a chance had I not been "warned", and I would not be writing this, because I would not be here. Up to this day, it remains a mystery to me "who" or "what" warned me. All I know is that it was not a real person and it was not a noise or a train signal, nothing physical.

HEAD, HEART AND GUT INTELLIGENCE: INSPIRATION

A special form of connection with the inner pulse of life and the universe, is inspiration. It is important to know what inspires you as it will reveal a great deal about who you are and what matters to you. Look at the people who have inspired you. Who are they and what do they stand for? What action would you take if you were like them? How would you lead your life?

Imagine the wind playing its tune through reeds or bamboo. Inspiration is like the wind playing through you. If you allow it to do so, if your essence is in resonance with the gentleness, the strength and the direction of the air, then who you are in your heart is reinforced and you can create the most beautiful sounds and unique melodies. It is as if you were connecting your individual pulse to the greater pulse of life.

In former times, when in need of spiritual advice or emotional support, people went to church or to a temple and prayed. The priestess spoke a wise oracle, or a shaman held a ritual. Today official religions in the West are losing their members. Many people prefer to consult a psychologist when they need help, others seek out a psychic or a life coach.

The yearning for the spiritual remains, and I believe there is a general trend towards spirituality without dogma or intermediary.

People are searching for a direct personal line to the divine, the Great Spirit, or whatever you will call this universal aspect. We want to experience first-hand how it feels and do not need others, who claim to know what is right for us. Inspiration is that direct line.

What we do need, sometimes, are instructions from someone experienced, who knows the way because they've been there. Like a good music teacher who passes on knowledge and techniques and can show me how to play my instrument, but cannot play in my place and will never express what I do. To remain with the image of music making, each person has a gift for a certain instrument, a liking for a certain type of music, and sometimes more than one. The same is true for our spiritual gifts and paths. There is not one way to the God-Field of universal intelligence, but as many, in my opinion, as there are human beings.

Inspiration is closely linked to wisdom. Wisdom means looking at things from a greater perspective, not being caught in current events. It is engaging completely in the actual moment, allowing time and space to expand so we can touch eternity, allowing not only the heart, but also the head to connect to insight. Wisdom is connected to love and does not judge lightly. It knows of greater connections and has acquired much knowledge. Over the years and through many experiences, the knowledge has been internalised and, together with serenity and benevolence, has been distilled to become wisdom. To hear this inner voice is what I wish for all of us. When you listen to it, you know what is right for everyone involved.

COHERENCE: OUR BRAINS CO-OPERATING

In the past up to now, achievement was closely related to the old mechanical way of thinking, making us believe we are a kind of top machine. It's been about working more and harder, using the head mainly, no matter what the price, no matter what it costs me.

Over the course of my muscial, artistic and coaching career I've uncovered a new approach. One that enables miracles and performing feats we never dreamt of as being possible for us. With this way of "performing" as opposed to "achieving" comes an element of flow, ease and gracefulness. When we see someone play an instrument on stage, we do not want to feel how difficult it is, technically or physically. A performance that inspires us also allows us to feel that it's easy.

The art of performing our best is not just about achieving a goal, it is going beyond, transforming things for the better, and thus bringing whatever it is we're doing to a higher level. It is using purpose and the bigger picture, as well as cooperating with life to accompish things we could never have imagined in our wildest dreams.

One of my clients had achieved more and succeeded beyond what most people ever reach, both in sports and in his professional life. He lost his job and then injured himself seriously doing sports. He was always out to achieve and push himself further and further, still under the infuence of his father, as he told me, and his upbringing, coming from an outdated view of the world. This client, who had achieved so much, could not appreciate it, and told me that he hated himself.

People with an outdated view on achievement, who reach the top, at the cost of their health or their personal life, are often driven by a lack of self-love. They have internalised what the majority of our society believes: I am only worth being loved if I achieve the maximum, and all that is expected from me. And not achieving or achieving less, means I am worthless. For this reason they will never ever win. Because it will never be enough. Break through this spiral now by creating a new view of the world and a new perspective on your own life.

In order to perform miracles rather than simply "achieve", we need to activate more of our inherent potential as human beings. That part which differentiates us from artificial intelligence and machines. This includes such skills as allowing ourselves to be inspired, using our intuition, following our instincts, being profoundly creative and feeling empathy. To access this it is crucial to love ourselves for who and what we are: a unique human being which only exists once in this universe. It is these qualities that enable us to accomplish great things, things no one else can, in our own unique way. Don't allow others to deter you.

To enable miracles we need to un-learn much of what we've learned growing up and over the course of our lives. It means utilising intelligence that goes way beyond that of our heads, and using skills that have been lying dormant, for various reasons, including because they are not deemed quantifiable, measurable and controllable.

We can then come up with a brilliant idea under the shower. High achievers of the old school check off things from their to-do list and find it difficult to let things rest.

They can only take a break when something is done. If, however, we listen to our gut or our intutition, asking us to take a break, we suddenly discover an unexpected shortcut or a new idea that is much better than the original one. A conscious break allows our minds to regroup und our brain to create new connections – a sign of higher intelligence as we will see.

We all know that we cannot think straight under stress, let alone act coherently. Taking breaks and using new tools that so far have been deemed esoteric or useless, because unrelated to business or figures, helps us create coherence. Stepping back and harmonizing our 3 brains head-heart-gut, will bring us into a whole new league of what is possible for us to create.

We have seen that Intelligence is about connections in the brain. The more connections, the more intelligent we are. If we take this a step further and connect the head, the heart and the gut, we will obviously be even more intelligent. This is a form of intelligence that is on an entirely new level, in a different league. We don't usually grow up learning about this. When our three brains are aligned, functioning together and, as a whole, we function at a higher level, more satisfied, fulfilled and connected with the world around us. We are also in better health.

The state in which head and heart are in sync, has been termed "coherence". I will extend this to include all of our brains: left and right, head, heart and gut. Coherence is commonly defined as "Clarity of thought, speech and emotional composure" and as "The quality of being orderly, consistent and intelligible." In terms of physics and waves/vibrations it is the "Synchronization or entrainment between multiple waveforms. A constructive waveform produced by two or more waves that are phase- or frequency-locked." Coherence between our brains means that they communicate, connect and interact with each other. It means all of those individual parts functioning as one whole, the sum greater than any or all of its parts.

What does this mean in practical terms? How do we go about creating coherence? In each of us, one brain or part of the brain tends to be more dominant, more active than the others. We not only perceive the world through different lenses, biased by our upbringing, cultural background, skills and taste, we also live in our own personal world, depending on which brain we are mostly centered in. Connecting to the world around us, the Field, in different ways, we draw different information, conclusions and experiences from there. WE are listening to different radio stations or watching different programs, to use the analogy we used above. Next time you argue with someone about what "really happened" or what is "really taking place", stop and remind yourself of this.

Let me illustrate how being centered in one or certain parts of our brains works for me. When something stressful happens, my first reaction is to gather all the facts I can, so that I can get a grip on the situation –

left part of the head brain. All the while, emotions are running high – heart, wanting me to react immediately – the gut. Some emotions will be vented, others not. Usually I express those that I feel to be appropriate.

To really come to terms with a challenging event or situation, I will need to have some time alone. I will need to get moving somewhere in nature, to activate my gut feelings, my gut brain, to then get an impulse for acting. Going for a walk, moving, helps me clear my head and allows my feelings to flow more freely. This is my way of synchronizing and connecting my brains. Once I've synchronised my three brains, I can move on to the next step, perhaps something I need or want to do as a result of this. Or I may find peace through insight and acceptance. I always sleep over any important decision. That enables me to calm down, get into a state of coherence, where my brains are functioning together, in their best possible way. Then I'm equipped to make a decision that is good for me, on all levels.

The interaction of the brains is a subtle form of interplay and interconnectedness. There are as many variations on this theme as there are individuals. It is up to you to find the exact balancing points and interfaces between your brains. To do so, observe yourself in times of stress, and get to know yourself.

The way we are centered can also quite easily be observed when we're learning something new. Learning becomes a lot easier and more natural if you know how your brains interact and where you are centered. Really anything you do becomes easier and less stressful if you know this part of yourself. You may find yourself more successful in presenting, in marketing your business just as in finding the right partner. You will perform at a higher level if you are coherent.

Whilst this is a profoundly personal journey, there are a number of practices and processes all of us can use that have been proven to work for many. As always, you will find your own preference, what works best for you.

CLEARING, CHARGING AND REWIRING OUR BRAINS

In order to create coherence, we first need to clear our brains, rather like emptying the garbage. If we don't, we may be all cluttered up, unable to receive the right information, insight or impulse.

Take a situation where you've been thinking a lot about an issue. Your thoughts are going around and around in your head. Your head is full. There is no room for anything new, for a new approach, insight or solution. Clearing your head will be the first necessary step in moving forward. A simple way of doing this is to write down everything that's on your mind. This allows your mind to let go for the moment, knowing nothing will get lost.

The same is true for emotions. For instance, when you lose your job, it can be quite emotional, in fact rather like losing someone you love. Before moving on and going for an interview with a possible new employer, you will need to reflect and clarify what happened. It is important to understand and accept this, come to terms with it, emotionally and mentally. If you burst into tears when you tell someone what happened, this is absolutely fine in a coaching session. However, your future employer would probably want nothing to do with you, rather like a new partner in life wants you to have come to grips with past relationships. Clearing allows us to move forward unimpeded by past experiences, and enables us to go beyond what we already know into new territory, so we don't have to recreate past failures and disasters.

Once our brains are "empty" or neutral, we can re-charge them and nourish them with positive energy: thoughts, feelings, insights and movement, or a combination thereof. When we do this, we rewire our brains. It is vital to understand that, at any given time, both our heads and our other brains can change. We can rewire them and it even appears that we can actually change our genome. Research has been done on this topic by scientists like Bruce Lipton, PhD.

If Buddhism and other forms of meditation showed me a way of dissociating myself from everyday life, from thoughts and emotions, in other words neutralizing my brains, they also left a void. For me, this was definitely not the end destination. It seemed like a first and necessary step, but not where I really wanted to be. Listening to music as a teenager, and later exploring inspiration in art and in everyday life, allowed me to experience something else, something I believe we all crave. It filled me up, the same way love does.

For the re-fill to be fulfilling and nourishing, I believe we need something more than self-centred energy, something more than our personal energy. This is called transpersonal in modern psychology and spirituality in traditional cultures. In former times, music and art, in other words culture, was an integral part of a cult. In mystical practices this energy can also flow through us in different forms of love, such as compassion, wisdom and inspiration.

Connecting to the Field of quantum physics, or God, if you like, is not only a way of tapping into a huge reservoir of information, it is also a way of not feeling isolated. This is what religion is about, a feeling of belonging, of being connected. We are beginning to understand that we are indeed all connected through the Field. This is not just a metaphor, it is meant literally on a physical, albeit microcosmic, level.

Let me mention one more way to connect and refuel: nature. Not surprising if we think that we are intrinsically part of nature. Although most of us have lost the awareness that this is so. Interestingly, doctors, especially in the UK, are beginning to prescribe spending time in nature besides art museums, music, dancing and meditating. Mainly for mental health, against stress and to strengthen our immune system. Against all the minor and major ailments of modern society, such as anxiety, depression and burnout, which are costing the state and companies horrendous amounts of money. Research has finally proven what we felt to be true on an experiential level all along: these are sustainable, easy to apply and very cost-effective ways of raising the level of well-being in our individual lives and society in general. While improving our well-being, they also enhance our level of performance.

CONNECTING WITH THE INNER PULSE OF LIFE

As we have seen, using all of our brains enables us to connect with our own inner pulse in the form of intuition, impulses and inspiration. There are as many ways of doing this as there are humans. It is important to find that which works for you, even if it doesn't work for anyone else. Don't allow others or false beliefs to stop you or to feel ashamed. Remember you are the expert on you, and only you. No teacher, coach or guru will ever be that.

There are, as always, stumbling blocks, and only practice makes perfect. As you embark on this path you may feel overwhelmed, insecure or anxious about making mistakes. Going into the unknown brings these feelings. In time, you will begin to develop your own sense of what "feels right" and I don't mean what feels the most comfortable or easy.

Our bodies can be good instruments for learning these processes. When something is in keeping with whom we are at a deeper level, our bodies react by relaxing and breathing deeper, for instance. When we want to go against our inner knowing, we become uptight and feel this in our bodies.

Here are some general practices that have been proven to work. They help us empty our minds and emotions to receive, connect and open up to the larger picture, the pulse of life. Find which ones works best for you.

MEDITATION

In brain scans, carried out with transcendental meditation, it has been shown that meditating synchronises the brain, connecting parts of the brain that normally don't cooperate. Psychiatrists, neurologists and molecular biologists have observed a number of positive effects of meditating on the functioning of the human brain and organism. Through regular meditation, feelings can be managed in a better way which in turn leads to reducing the negative effect of stress hormones. Thus, according to the current state of research, meditation is capable of influencing inflammatory illnesses, the immune system and even the ageing of cells.

Relaxation techniques and forms of meditation help us empty and clear the mind and we can also utilise them to rewire our brains, creating a new lens through which to look at life. This neutral lens can more readily adapt to who I am, and to what I would like to create that really matters to me.

When we talk about meditation, most people think of sitting quietly with our legs crossed in a yogi posture. Yet, sitting by a river and gazing into the water, allowing your mind to empty and your thoughts to roam freely, is also a form of meditation. Just as going for a walk in the woods can be, or in fact anything that brings us entirely into the present moment. This also allows us to step back from the grip of overthinking or being overly emotional.

When I started on my quest to find spirit in music, art and later in our modern Western world, I tried many different forms of meditation. A lot of them gave me really bad headaches, pushing me to explore further. Looking back on this, I would say that being still and quiet, intensified the use of my head and my emotions. Having suffered some head injuries and dealing with an emotionally challenging childhood, these unresolved issues and traumas were triggered, causing me to experience bad headaches, rather than blissful peace and tranquility.

My first successful meditation was a guided inner journey. Here the body lies or sits still whilst the head is occupied with listening and making sense of what the voice guiding you is asking you to do. There is a form of inner movement and natural flow which allowed my head, the analytical part that is, to let go and focus on what was happening. The voice is like a stream, moving steadily and gently.

Meanwhile, interested in how different forms of meditation affect us, I have tried many other forms, from Zen and Yoga, to colours and chakras, to music. I can now "play" with what is the most appropriate at the moment. Don't stop if the first form of meditation you try doesn't work or if it doesn't have the desired effect.

MINDSET

Successful top athletes use mind techniques to enhance their performance. We all know that how we think about a particular situation influences how we perform. If I think it's possible, it will be easier to reach a certain goal than if I believe it to be impossible. There are always reasons to believe one or the other, by the way.

Our mindset can furthermore be effective in dealing with pain, depression and anxiety. While top athletes usually visualise the desired outcome, we don't always know what this looks like for us. So sometimes, it's a good idea to imagine the feeling we will have when we have achieved what we desire, rather than the specific result.

We can use affirmations in addition to visualizing. Simply affirming "I am rich", "I am healthy" etc, will, however, not work unless you totally believe it. The wording is essential, as much as actually feeling the words. A simple technique I use with my clients is a good starting point: go to a place in your mind where you already experienced feeling rich or healthy, anchor it, then visualise your present situation and allow that particular positive feeling of richness or health to flow into it.

Just as it's taken many years and tens or even hundreds of thousands of hours to engrave our current beliefs and thoughts into our brains, it will take more than once to engrave a new pattern. Remember this before giving up too soon.

IMAGES AND IMAGERY

Images have a noticeable effect on our bodies and minds. Research has shown that whatever we look at has an immediate effect on our entire system, one we cannot control. Images influence the stress level in our bodies or can help us relax. Remember the reaction to images in the context of gut feelings?

What is really interesting here, is that our systems don't distinguish between imagined images and what we see in the real world. Whatever image we imagine or look at affects the functioning of our bodies, i.e. our breath, heart rate, muscle tension etc., as well as how we feel emotionally. We can use this in a simple yet highly effective way, by imagining something beautiful, peaceful, loving. We can also surround ourselves with pictures and art that have a positive effect on our well-being on all levels: body, mind and heart. And, we can even use images as a form of energy, rather like a coffee to wake up, sweet music to fall asleep, a smell to appease etc. They transport information and energy, with which our bodies and minds can resonate, releasing necessary hormones and energy within us.

There are images everywhere, surrounding us. We live in a highly visual world. It is worth taking a moment to become conscious of how these images affect us and our well-being.

Looking at a work of art of your choice could be your way of consciously exploring its effect on you. Try this: sit down in front of your favorite picture, work of art or photograph. Look at it in a focused and relaxed way. Feel how your breathing changes as well as your heart rate and other physiological parameters. This can go either way: you can relax or tense up. You can thus explore the effect of any image on you personally. Does it change how you're feeling?

Both pictures and music can activate sources of energy that are not accessible through words alone. Images access intelligence in a much more fundamental and wholistic way than words or ideas can, as they speak to more ancient parts of the brain in a more inter-connected way. They provide an abundance of information not accessible through our rational minds. Modern science even contends that intelligence works in images.

The right side of your brains in our heads stores all the data and memories we ever have. These are filtered by our analytical mind, the left side of the brain, so that we can function in everyday life and not be overwhelmed and flooded with too much data. Images, as well as certain activities such as engaging in painting, music and other artistic activities, actually give us access to this otherwise locked data bank. And by accessing the stored data, we can obtain information about a situation which by far exceeds that of the conscious mind. This is very useful when we are confronted with having to make a decision or finding creative solutions.

Because images can store a lot of information, they can further help us memorise facts. According to neuroscientists, we are normally able to memorise only five characteristics or facts at a time. Memory trainers use images and stories to remember an endless row of facts.

Images can thus also serve as guides and inspiration in difficult situations. Besides utilizing images as sources of information and of inspiration, we can explore our own images regarding a topic, a question or a problem.

An antidote to the flood of external stimuli, by the way, is a form of meditation where I close my eyes and see the colour black. I keep my focus on the black and not the images or thoughts that cross my mind. It's a good exercise for learning to focus and it empties our senses.

SIGNS

Sometimes we are desperate to connect with our inner pulse, with life itself, and this pressure is precisely what makes it impossible for our brains to function coherently. It is easier said than done to let go in some cases, as we all know.

This is where a little help from outside can be beneficial. What if asking the universe for a sign does actually work in some mysterious way? If we are connected to the Field, where all information is stored and accessible, and our perception is a certain lens through which we draw this information, perhaps it is indeed possible to read in the Field as in a book and to understand its message.

The most important aspect of reading signs and the most difficult to handle, is the interpretation when there is a lot of pressure or expectation. It's best to look at signs as synchronistic reflections of what is going on inside of you, a kind of mirror that reflects what you think and feel.

Here's an example. Getting towards the end of this book and wondering about how to go about publishing it, I was pondering this question. In fact, it was on my mind constantly for a few days: Should I self-publish, find an agent or…? Talking to a friend, she told me that while she was working on her book, ideas for online courses kept coming up and she was writing them down in parallel. While I have also been wanting to do online courses, this was not happening with me. And I couldn't will it to happen. The next time I was working on my book, the idea of a workbook kept coming up and I realised I had actually had that idea before but had forgotten about it.

Now, I picked it up again and started to really work on it. This had an added benefit of making me confident enough to believe I will be able to promote this book in business. Another sign came in a completely different form and shape. Whilst I was wondering what to do, driving in my car, I looked over to the right at a parked van. I noticed one word, on its own, with no other text or image around it: "kindle". Kindle is the e-book format that enables people to self-publish on amazon. To me that was a sign, as well as what my friend had said.

Signs come in many forms: images, words, thoughts other people have about a situation, a book title, a film… You will feel when it clicks, when it's more than just wishful thinking. Take signs into account, but use common sense as well. Not everything we see is a sign and needs to be taken seriously.

FLOW

A particular form of meditation involving our bodies and our emotions is peak physical performance, such as mountain climbing. Requiring our full concentration, this is termed "flow" and is a state also reached when creating artistically or during any activity that completely allows us to get lost in what we are doing. In flow, we are utterly focused on the activity we are involved in. All other thoughts, emotions or concerns are forgotten. The state of flow is particularly powerful in emptying and filling us up, because it involves our minds, hearts and bodies. If you have trouble with meditation practices as such, find an activity that allows you to experience flow.

CREATING ART

One way to experience flow is through expressing ourselves artistically. Whilst many of us have heard about the benefits of meditation, fewer of us know about the profound benefits of artistic expression. Creating art is another way to access a meditative state of mind and the profound healing it brings. When creating artistically, we get totally involved in the process. We step outside of our "normal" everyday thought patterns and focus on both expressing who we are on a deeper level, non-verbally, and finding ways to do so. We tap into our creativity. It is a profound way of connecting with who we are at our core, independent of others. In creating art, we forget about negative feelings and create distance to our often anxious thoughts, connecting with our true selves. While we are creating, we experience flow and freedom from what is going on in our lives. We access a quiet, deeper part of ourselves.

MUSIC

The benefits of music on our well-being and our bodies have been widely researched. Listening to music is one of the easiest ways to create resilience and a state of relaxation, or to simply tune into a positive and uplifting kind of energy. Research shows that when you listen to music you like, your brain releases dopamine, a "feel-good" neurotransmitter. Listening to music you enjoy decreases levels of the stress hormone cortisol in your body, counteracting the effects of chronic stress. This is an important finding since stress is by far the greatest known cause for illnesses and disease. It is also the cause for not being able to perform at our best.

A study showed that students who listened to relaxing classical music for 45 minutes before turning in slept significantly better than students who listened to an audiobook or did nothing different from their normal routine.

More than 350 million people suffer from depression around the world. Against that background, another study demonstrated that music can benefit patients with depressive symptoms, depending on the type of music. Meditative sounds and classical music lifted people up, but techno and heavy metal brought people down even more. Research also found that music therapy and pre-recorded music reduced pain on the condition that the selection be either classical pieces, meditative music or songs of the patient's choosing.

How does this work? Music can create coherence, synchronizing our brains: the head, the heart and the belly. When we listen to music, we use a simple phenomenon which we have talked about before: resonance.

Listening to music with a slow pulse has an immediately relaxing effect through the phenomenon of resonance. We snychronise our brains and heartbeats to the pulse of the music. There are different wavelengths in our brain for different states of consciousness: alpha, delta and theta, all of them being forms of deep relaxation and hypnosis. The heart rate varies according to rest/exercise/stress etc. Music with 60 beats a minute would appear to be a good starting point to relax. This will happen whether we like the music or not, simply because of the resonance of what we hear.

In both music and art I have experienced how my creative energy can be used to plug into the current of the universe, connecting me to my heart and soul and moving into dimensions of existence that are mystical, heart-warming and fulfilling. Having first experienced these states as a teenager through listening to music as well as playing music myself, I learned to label them much later as ecstasy and trance. Both states are more commonly known to be reached through religious or spiritual practice in shamanism and ancient tribal ceremonies. Or through drugs, both healing and hallucinatory.

Traveling through Europe at the young age of 16, I landed in Amsterdam, where I was offered some hashish to try. Here was my chance to explore further what I had already experienced in music. Everybody told me how it made listening to music and dancing, as well as colours, much more intense. However, for me it was a let-down.

I felt that what I was able to experience without any kind of drug was more powerful – perhaps because induced by myself. How do you get into a state of ecstasy and trance without drugs? I knew there was music, I didn't know about all the rest, like shamanism etc. This was to become an exploration of a lifetime in conjunction with my artistic endeavors.

Recently scientists observed how a brain was firing away in lots of areas at the same time while the person was playing a musical instrument. It seemed like a firework going off in the brain. This would explain the feelings I had.

Music also enhances intelligence. About 30 years ago a study was done in Swiss schools that demonstrated how students who had more music lessons than the average schedule, and therefore less maths and language, were as good in maths and language as those with more lessons per week in those subjects.

If music activates our brain in the head this way, we now know it will also have a massive effect on our other brains, as they are deeply connected. Different types of music affect our brains in different ways. They can impact the gut first, or the heart first, and then the head. This means that there is an entire art here as to finding the right music to enable healing and coherence. Ancient tribes and ancient Greeks knew of this effect of music and actively utilised it for healing.

Bearing in mind that a healthy heart does not beat absolutely rigidly and regularly like a machine, we need to think about what kind of music will best serve our purpose here with regards to regenerating, up-lifting and improving our health and well-being, as well as creating coherence of the brains for top performance. Certainly, any music where the beat is generated mechanically through a computer will not be beneficial. This excludes most of modern pop music, except singer songwriter music that is unplugged. It also excludes many other modern genres like heavy metal.

I suggest you try classical, country or meditation music – beware here too, though, because much of modern meditation music is computer-generated.

NATURE

Spending time in nature is one of the most effective ways to regain well-being and it comes at no price. Scottish doctors are prescribing nature and the Japanese practice of "forest bathing" is scientifically proven to improve your health. We are part of nature and have forgotten this vital connection to our own health. By going into nature, we reconnect to who we are, to our roots, on a genetic level.

What's more, scientists are finding that plants and animals are far more intelligent than we have given them credit for in our materialistic view of the world. A movie has been produced solely about the intelligence of trees and how they communicate with each other. What used to be termed esoteric and thereby devalued, is now becoming the object of scientific research. Science is bridging the gap between ancient mystical knowledge and our intellectual intelligence.

Let me take this idea a step further: if trees are intelligent beings, so are other plants, animals and perhaps even stones. And if these beings represent a specific form of intelligence, they could be regarded as being like the morphogenetic fields described by Sheldrake. We could tune into them for information and knowledge, just like the way shamans connect to their totem animals and plants for guidance. We are using physical elements of plants and animals to heal us. Why not the "spirits" of plants? Homeopathy works with this field idea. In fact, in the age of information, this seems rather appropriate: learning to use the information given by plants and nature.

According to scientific research, walking barefoot on the ground strengthens the immune system and leads to less infections or colds. In parallel, children who don't have enough contact with dirt, with the earth, are much more prone to diseases affecting the immune system such as asthma and allergies.

It seems vital for us to connect to our environment, not just physically but also on an emotional level, as we will see further on. Connecting to nature can be just as important as connecting to others. Let us remember this next time before cutting ourselves off from nature by wearing ear-phones.

PURPOSE

*"The two most important days in your life are the day
you are born and the day you find out why."*
Mark Twain

If you're looking for the most powerful way to activate
all of your potential, I believe it is through purpose
and love. Purpose is one of the most sustainable ways to
create coherence and well-being, as well as enabling us to
perform miracles. Finding our very own meaning in life
and creating what matters, engages all of who we are, all
of our different brains. It draws on the depth of unused
potential, because it is the strongest driving force we
have, besides love. It has the added benefit of connecting
us to the world around us, as purpose is often connected
to the world, and not a selfish endeavour just for my
own good. Many people are likely to benefit from our
purpose or mission in life. This activates the "miracle
potential".

*"You don't become happy by pursuing happiness. You
become happy by living a life that means something,"*
says Harold S. Kushner.

Research has shown that having purpose and meaning
in life increases overall well-being and life satisfaction,
improves mental and physical health, enhances resiliency
and self-esteem and decreases the chances of depression.

So, it should be noted that to be happy in life isn't always enough; it's more important to have meaning in life. Meaning is not only about transcending the self, but also about transcending the present moment. While happiness is an emotion felt in the here and now, it ultimately fades away, as do all emotions.

FORMS OF LOVE

Next time you or someone you know struggles with depression, perhaps think about why we are constantly encouraged to take prescription medication, when heartfulness techniques actually show more promise. Love is the greatest connector of our brains. We all know the saying that love knows no boundaries and that it can override any obstacle. Love mobilises mental, emotional and physical strength: the proverbial mother who can lift a car to save her child.

We all associate different feelings and ideas with love. Many of us have been hurt and have closed our hearts to this incredible source of energy in an effort to protect ourselves. So, whilst for some, talking about love is fine, for others it may be easier to access this reservoir through other forms of the same basic energy. This is why we will look at different forms of love to activate all of what is inside of us. Chose that which resonates most, that which seems easiest for you to feel.

GRATITUDE

Scientists have discovered that feelings of gratitude can actually change our brains. When life is full of challenges and nothing seems right, it may seem impossible to feel gratitude. But when you think of it, there is always something to be grateful for. Let your feelings guide you. What springs to mind spontaneously? What are you grateful for? Perhaps you've just recovered from an illness and you're grateful just to be alive? Or there is someone who has always stayed by your side and supported you through difficult times? Or simply a beautiful place in nature, where you can relax and feel at home. We can feel gratitude for being alive, opening our eyes in the morning, having a roof over our heads, food on our table and many other seemingly small blessings.

If you cannot think of something to be grateful for at the present moment, perhaps because you're in a crisis that is so overwhelming that it colours your every thought and feeling, go back in time. To when you were a child. Was there a simple moment of bliss, where you were entirely present, happy to be alive, engrossed in an activity or with someone you loved?

Whatever you're grateful for, allow this feeling to build as you think about it. Then allow your mind and heart to "wander" to other things that evoke similar feelings. You will notice that, in time, this becomes easier and that there will be more and more things to be grateful for. Start with the easiest and then extend to the more "difficult" aspects of your life.

FORGIVENESS

As we move through life, we experience small and large losses, hurts and pains. Most of us have never learned to deal with these. We either push them away so as not to have to feel the pain, or we get overwhelmed, depressed, angry and stuck in these emotions. We allow our hearts to fill up with hurtful emotions such as shame, anger, hurt and pride.

What we rarely realise is the extent to which these emotions tarnish the "purity and innocence" of the hearts with which we were born. As our hearts become "blemished" and full, they lose their freshness and resilience.

Because anger and resentment are powerful poisons, it is a good idea to empty our hearts, to cleanse them, just as we clean our bodies and clear our homes and workspace of what we don't want or need any more.

The most powerful way to do this, and perhaps the most difficult in some cases, is the act of forgiving. Once we realise that holding a grudge actually hurts us more than it does the person we hold a grudge against, we are perhaps motivated to give it a try. This is neither a religious nor an esoteric act. It is common sense. Especially, if we understand that forgiving someone does not necessarily mean supporting and endorsing that person's behaviour.

If I forgive, I allow something larger than my limited self to take over. Me and my little ego think that I'm right: right in holding a grudge, in judging the other person. Love, as always, offers a larger picture. Who am I to judge someone? Do I know what that person feels, thinks, experiences? It offers us a different perspective, one that in the end will enhance my well-being and my capacity to perform at a high level.

Forgiving is an act of kindness. To yourself, your soul and body, as well as the others involved. Our heads will most likely think that we are right in holding a grudge and will not budge. However, once it realises that the feelings caused by these thoughts, impeach our full potential, we can lure the head into coming onto our side, to help us find ways to forgive, or at least clear the way for it to happen. We can allow love to come into a situation which, in turn, can lead to forgiveness.

Perhaps adopting the view that we are both right AND wrong could be a good way forward. Thinking back to the blue and red ball, we understand that we only see one side of the coin, not the other. There are always, yes, always, more sides to situations or a problem.

We have all heard the saying: beauty is in the eye of the beholder. The same is true for anything. Love is also in the eye of the beholder. We can choose to look at a person through a lens of anger and fear, or one of love and forgiveness.

In this sense, love doesn't make us blind, but rather

makes us see! You cannot change another person by loving them, but you can create a space where that person's potential, strength and true nature can blossom, by giving them love.

ACCEPTANCE

Accepting people for who they are is especially difficult when faced with hurtful or destructive behaviour, or when someone is unhappy and we feel we know what they need to be better. Reminding ourselves that each one of us is unique, will help here. We will never fully understand another person in their feelings, motivations and behaviour. There will always be something that eludes us. Accepting others is a choice. Like love. I can choose to accept you for what and who you are, even if I don't understand. Accepting, again, is not endorsing everything you do. I can accept you and not support your behaviour.

COMPASSION

If we are all connected through an invisible field of energy, we can look at what is outside to reflect on what is inside of us. In psychology this is called mirroring. For instance, if someone annoys us, rather than just putting it all on that person, we look inside ourselves and recognise the annoying aspect to be an aspect of our own personality that we have trouble accepting. By reflecting, we no longer need to fight the person outside, but rather accept the trait as an inherent part of ourselves, therefore accepting it in others.

In Buddhism compassion is the highest form of enlightenment and love. Compassion allows us to feel with others without getting sucked in or pulled over. Compassion is based on the understanding that what you are feeling and experiencing is part of the human condition.

FEELING CONNECTED

It is said that isolation and loneliness account for a huge part of current mental illnesses. Loneliness is not only about being alone, it is about being and feeling separate. When we perceive ourselves as being cut off from the rest of the world, whether in a crowd of people or on a desert island, we are lonely.

At work, people feel under pressure to achieve and compete with each other. This leads to a lack of genuine communication and feelings, commonly regarded as non-professional. Some companies are beginning to realise that employees who can express their feelings, perform better, are healthier and more loyal.

Online there is a trend to show only the great and successful parts of ourselves. We can sometimes be vulnerable, but we should not be different. When we get attacked online, our bodies and minds react in the same way as they do offline. These feelings need to be addressed and tended to in both cases or they can lead to serious problems.

Apart from these cases of feeling separate, we are sometimes physically separate from others. In all of these cases, as in the case of conflicts which are also about separation, it is a good idea to consciously connect.

Sometimes it is enough to realise that we are all interconnected on a physical level, as with the Field that connects everything and everybody. Did you know studies that researched our blood and the genetic material of different cultures, tribes, continents and ethnical identity, show us all to be a huge melting pot? No-one has one ethnic background. We all belong to different ethnic groups without knowing it. This means we are connected on a very physical level.

On an emotional level, it is important to realise that we are also related and connected, whether we like it or not, whether we believe it or not. Remember the phenomenon of resonance? We vibrate with each other, always. Many situations can be solved through creating conscious connections. We can connect with our different brains. The information given here helps the head to connect. Emotionally, it is the heart that can best do this. Take time to feel connected: with family and friends, with colleagues and at your workplace, but also with nature and culture.

When you have a conflict, connect to what is creating it, see it as a part of yourself, a mirror you're looking into. Another way to connect is by realizing you are partly responsible through the act of co-creation.

Connect to your feelings, to your creativity, your perception, to who you are. Connect with what is around you, the present moment, touch a tree or a stone. Feeling connected to yourself, through whatever act or in whatever way, really helps when you're feeling lonely. Try it!

CREATE WHAT MATTERS

Having explored who we are on an individual level, learned about our human potential that has been lying dormant, it is now time to activate all of it and put it into practice.

This process of creating is much like that of growing a tree. Intention is like the seed in planting. Watering it, putting it in the right soil, is doing anything and everything I possibly can at that moment to bring it into existence. In my experience, there often comes a break after this. Germination begins, when I let go and allow the universe to step in. This may happen fairly quickly, like within days, or it may take decades. I have experienced all of these time frames.

Then life, when we least expect it, offers us opportunities. These are often not in the form we would envisage them, sometimes not even obvious as something we would want. Luckily, we have our different brains we have learned to trust by now. There is a gut feeling about opportunities. We just know this is the right moment and the right offer. The head may find good reasons against it. Often, the amount of fear equals the energy of desire.

If it is something we've longed for and worked towards, deeply connected to who we are, it can be really scary. There is just so much at stake. Usually, the anticipated joy is a little bit stronger than the associated fear.

Every time I went on stage to perform in public, just before, I would think: why am I doing this to myself? Why did I ever agree to this? I was terrified, with sweaty hands and a pounding heart. Over the years, I learned that this was part of the deal. I learned to go with this energy. For that is what it is: an incredible burst of energy that we'd like to control, but cannot. I knew that once I was on stage and started playing, the energy would go into performing, into expressing and touching the audience. After a few notes, I was away on a huge wave of energy. And after the concert, I was so exhilarated, happy and deeply satisfied. I knew why I had done it!

Creating what matters is a process much like parenting, bringing with it all the stages of a baby growing up. After giving birth to what matters to you, raising it into a "grown-up", it's time to let it go out into the world on its own and for it to find its place.

ENTERING THE CREATIVE ZONE: OUR SACRED SPACE

There is a kind of inner space, a zone, where the magic of creation and inventions happen. It is a place you cannot access directly and willfully. It is beyond our conscious efforts. What we can do is create the right frame and conditions for it to happen. For this, we need to step out of our busy lives, full of distractions. This could well be one of the most challenging aspects of creating meaning in your life.

Most of us have learned that we achieve by working hard. While there are definitely things we need to do to manifest our dreams, there are probably just as many times when we need to do nothing. This doesn't however mean watching tv or hanging out with friends.

We can only access the creative zone when we are alone, when our mind is busy with something, like taking a shower, folding the washing, cleaning, going for a walk. But not when we are challenged or extremely focused.

When we look into water or at clouds, watching their movement and changing forms, we are busy enough, but at the same opening up the border between our conscious and the subconscious mind. We can enter into the huge reservoir of information not accessible to our normal "doing-active" modus. We access this zone in meditation, in music, in flow and artistic creation through images and when we go for walks in nature.

We all have places where we feel good, activities that allow us to express without thinking and things we love doing. These are crucial for recharging our batteries, reconnecting with our inner selves, our own inner pulse. We have seen how, through listening to music, meditating and other activities, we access and activate our full potential. These activities allow us to empty our minds, reconnect with our inner selves and come into contact with our essence and our purpose.

Now it is time to express this, to bring our purpose into the world. In order to do this, we need to create spaces, rituals and routines in everyday life. We need a kind of sanctuary where no one and nothing matters but ourselves.

Rituals, just like music, art or meditation are gateways, allowing us to enter other dimensions. They prepare the way, giving a kind of signal that now other things are possible than those in everyday life. When conducting a ritual, the body experiences through the senses that something extraordinary is happening; we tap into other aspects of ourselves. We need places where we can experience the feeling of being at one with who we are and why we're here. Places where we receive answers or hints to important questions in our lives.

It may be a good idea to physically create a space where you can meditate in whatever form is right for you. A place that is always there when you need it. Your sanctuary just for yourself, to reflect, create, or simply do nothing. A playroom, a breathing space. If you don't have space in your home, this can be in nature. Go to your favorite tree, sit by the water undisturbed to meditate.

I call these creative spaces sacred. Why sacred? There is something profoundly holy about entering them. This is the core of creation, an alchemistic process, where straw turns into gold metaphorically speaking. We connect to something much greater, encountering spirit and inspiration.

People used to go to church or a temple to experience this connection. And some of us still do. But we can also enter these mystic zones of inspiration anywhere in nature, or by looking at a work of art or listening to music.

When you step into the void, into the unknown, the big mystery, you allow the cycle of creation to return. Letting go, stepping into the unknown, can be the first step in creating your next work of art, project or meaningful pursuit.

VISION AND FOCUS

Quantum physics tells us that the particles of physical matter exist as a virtual state in the form of waves. These waves become particles and, as such, physical reality through our perception of them. Translated into everyday life, this means: where our focus goes, is where our reality unfolds.

Think of it this way: do you remember a time where a specific topic was on your mind, such as having children, traveling to a special holiday resort? And then suddenly everyone around you was pregnant or you saw photos of the place you were wanting to go to, heard stories about it? This is how this phenomenon works. Our focus brings these external reflections of what we are focusing on. There is definitely a connection between our thoughts and perceptions, what is on our mind, and what we perceive in the outer world. This connection will help us materialise our dreams and visions.

We tend to think of a vision as an image or a series of images which will guide us to realizing our dreams, that we see with our inner eyes. This is indeed a powerful guide in the creation process, one that connects us to our innermost essence and feeds us along the way.

Let us also consider vision as a way of seeing. Physically we have poor or excellent vision (or anything in between). By the same token we can have good or mediocre vision as regards the perception of our lives and the situation we are in. This is closely related, but not exactly the same as perspective. A perspective arises through vision, through the way we chose to perceive.

What if we opted to regard our current life situation as being perfect – not in an absolute sense. Not having enough money is, of course, by no means a perfect situation. But perhaps it is the perfect situation to motivate me to take the necessary steps towards a more fulfilling life. I suggest we look at our current situation in life as being perfect for ourselves, from a higher perspective. One we need to grow into at times, that is not obvious on the surface, that is hidden. For this, we need to be willing to not be right all the time, to let go of resentment or hurt or anger, as much as to trust life and the universe we live in.

We have seen that our focus is part of the process of creation.

We manifest and create what we focus on. Remember

this when confronted with what you don't want. Always bring your focus back to what you truly want. Many of us tend to focus on what we do not have or do not like. By so doing, we reinforce precisely that, because that is where we put our energy. As energy follows focus, we keep manifesting the same thing over and over again. Learning to see through the eyes of love can be crucial in this context. It will allow us to step back and change perspective, whether it is self-love, gratefulness or forgiveness.

Loving ourselves and our lives the way it is right now, is one way of creating the space for things to change and stop reinforcing what we don't want. Matter can thus re-structure. Some teachers of quantum physics propose going into a complete void, focusing on the void in order to allow matter to regroup. I think this is also a valid approach. Whatever works. I find it's easier to focus on something rather than nothing.

Love allows things to be the way they are, without focusing on anything in particular; it's a wide open space, without fixation. Fighting against some aspect of myself, life or another person, actually gives it lots of energy, helping it to stay alive, to keep re-manifesting.

Images can be used like external forms of visions, ways to visualise what is inside of us. Both inner and outer images can act as guides, orientation, inspiration and sources of information. Allowing us to see the larger picture and to change perspective, they represent a highly effective tool of creation.

THE POWER OF THOUGHTS, WORDS AND SOUND TO CREATE

A good friend contacted me yesterday in total despair. She is what we laughingly and lovingly call an addict of spiritual readings, whether astrology, cards, or clairvoyant. Yesterday, a consultant told her that this year there was no money, no love and also that her health was going to be bad.

What, may you ask, does this have to do in a book about creating meaning and well-being? When we go to see doctors, whether alternative or traditional, Western or Eastern, spiritual or hands on, they all have an impact on our healing process. What they say, their tone of voice, their message and the way they tell us, all have an immense impact on how we heal.

What any kind of consultant, or person we know for that matter, says about who we are and what we are doing, has a huge impact. Self-fulfilling prophecies do exist. Often, we are not even aware of them, because they have become inherent beliefs. They will be like the proverbial pink elephant, the one we try to not think of. And it takes discipline to ban them from our minds and hearts.

Luckily, we do not depend on anyone outside ourselves. We have the power to choose who and what is best for us, who will best support us in the path we have chosen. There are, I believe, as many paths to healing and well-being as there are people on this earth. There are also many, many healing methods and variations thereof, and what will be beneficial for one, will not be so for another. What works largely depends on our own beliefs, the environment we live in and what we've come to accept as possible. It is vital to bear this in mind.

People who seek guidance or professional advice take what they hear very seriously, sometimes much more so than we could ever imagine and often for many years to come. This is probably one of the reasons that some people don't even like to consult fortune-tellers or doctors, because they're afraid of what they're going to hear and how it's going to affect them. And rightly so!

Let us also bear this in mind when we talk to ourselves, internally, in our minds, as well as when we talk about ourselves to others. Many of us, with the marketing boom, have learned to talk a certain way when describing our jobs and what we do. We present ourselves in the best possible way. This is actually quite clever. The universe is listening. If I say I'm really good at…, this will reinforce my performance every time. The same is true for my health. If I talk a lot about how bad I feel, this will focus my energy on this aspect. In dealing with people who are suffering from depression, anxiety or burnout, I noticed that they are always talking about themselves, their lives, their situation in an extremely negative way. This does not allow for a more positive energy to enter into the situation. It just perpetuates more of the same. There is a fine line between communicating your feelings and reinforcing negative feelings and pains.

A friend of mine was told many years ago he would

be working in the pharmaceutical industry, which at the time seemed highly unlikely. The psychic also told him he had the gift to heal others, but that he wouldn't be using it in this lifetime. This man really did work for the pharmaceutical industry for about 30 years and then lost his job. He doesn't work at all now and he doesn't use his healing abilities which he proved he had on several occasions. To this day, he has in his mind what the psychic told him. But who are we to tell people what their purpose is in this life? Would he be healing, rather than looking after his garden, not unhappily I may add, had he been told otherwise?

We can use words to build or destroy, to empower or weaken. We can use words to get across who we are, what we do and how we do it.

Another aspect of words is their sound. The world, according to the Bible and other spirtual myths, was created through word-sound. The use of your voice as a positive instrument is certainly worth exploring. I have actually helped people get a job by enabling them to use their voices in a more suited and more pleasant manner. A client once contacted me to help him in the application process. He was getting invited to interviews and then didn't get any further. The feedback was that he didn't come across as being confident enough. He's a lawyer.

So, to help build his confidence, we worked on the wording of his answers to interview questions and on understanding his strengths. During this process it became increasingly clear to me that we would need to work on his voice, too. It was rather high pitched and slightly broken, so no matter what he said, with this tone of voice he would not come across as being confident and strong. The first and greatest challenge was for him to hear this. Then I gave him some simple exercises to connect with another part of his voice, the deeper one. He practiced and got the job he wanted. We didn't change who he was, we just made it possible for another part of him that was somewhat hidden and unexpressed, to come forth and be heard.

Our voice is a very powerful instrument of creation and it's connected to who we are in our very essence. Vocation and voice have the same latin stem: vocare = to call. So, our voice is connected to our calling.

There are two aspects to using our voice: one is listening, the other expressing. Listening is connected to knowing who I am, expressing is communicating this to the world around me. One needs the other to be balanced and fulfilled. As we explore who we are, our voice plays a significant part and can support us in creating what we want.

STORIES – REWRITING OUR LIVES

Stories can be powerful tools, just like images, to rewire our brains. The wisdom of ancient ages was passed on to future generations through stories, not technical explanations or ideas. When coaching people who have lost their job or have become ill, it is worth to first look at the story as perceived by my clients. In this story there is often an aspect of being a victim, sometimes there is already a hint of how the person actually co-created the situation, e.g. "I've been wanting to change jobs for the past 2 years".

By finding out more about the situation and how it unfolded, by getting background information like "I was unhappy there because what I really want is…", allows them to switch perspective. All of a sudden, life is on their side by making them redundant and giving them the opportunity to do what they really wanted in the first place, and now even with the support of a coach.

Many people, after having gone through an ordeal, can see how this unexpected and uninvited situation, triggered something positive in their lives. Just like me getting sick several years ago and discovering the aspect of self-love.

By re-writing our story, we take back our power, we come out as the "heroes" of our lives, one who has mastered ordeals and hardship and has overcome obstacles. This strengthens rather than weakens us. Many of my clients, at the end of the coaching, tell me they have (re)gained their self-confidence. They feel empowered. When they come, they usually feel weak, powerless, and incapable.

TRUE MAGIC: THE PULSE OF THINGS AND WE ARE ONE

We have seen that there is something like a mysterious inner pulse to who we are, to what we are creating, our inner sense of timing, as well as an external pulse that we encounter in signs and events in the outer world. When both pulses, inner and outer, come together, there is synchronicity. This is experienced as coincidence or fate – depending on the nature of the event and our beliefs.

When inner and outer pulse coincide to form synchronistic events, it feels like you're in flow with life, yourself and the world around you. This is a sure sign that you're on track. And it feels like magic. This is the stuff miracles are made of.

THE PULSE OF THINGS AND WE ARE ONE

Can you hear it,
the breath of water?
Can you hear them,
clouds floating by?
Can you hear
the songs of your soul?

Hear it, see it, touch it…
the pulse of things as they unfold.

OUR SECRET POTENTIAL

The pulse of things and we are one.
Can you see it,
the sound of snow?
Can you see them,
stones growing old?
Can you see
the beauty of your soul?

Hear it, see it, touch it…
the pulse of things as they unfold.
The pulse of things and we are one.

Can you touch them,
the words we spoke?
Can you touch them,
our hidden thoughts?
Can you touch
love at its core?

Hear it, see it, touch it…
the pulse of things as they unfold.
The pulse of things and we are one.

© *Tessa Richter, 2013*

TO THE MOON AND BEYOND

ast year I was asked what wisdom I would share with 15 to 20 year-olds. This was to be part of a book dedicated to that age group. I read what others wrote and found it inspiring and then realised I didn't want to give any kind of advice, even if it was good advice, and I didn't want to be lecturing or talking at young people.

Traditionally, the elders told stories to the young ones, and that is what I opted for. Here is my story, the best way I can illustrate everything I have talked about in this book. It will help you understand what I mean. At the age of 60 I started a completely new career, one I could never ever have dreamed up. This was life's way of showing me that we can create what matters at absolutely any age.

MIRACLES

hen I was 15, life seemed intense, full of possibilities, but also hard to fathom. I felt like an outsider, having grown up in many different places, in different cultures, with three different languages. And, although I was tested highly gifted, I felt inadequate, unable to perform to the expectations of those around me. I spent almost 40 years trying to fit in, to be like everyone else.

I wish someone had been there to hold my hand, to support me. But, perhaps, I had to develop my own understanding of myself and my own way of dealing with life. One essential thing I learned was to co-operate with life as it is.

Here is my story of how life took me by the hand and together we went to the moon and beyond. I achieved more than I ever would have imagined possible. And I'm finally beginning to feel that I belong. There's not one group, one family, but many.

Music, when I was 15, was an inner home for me. When playing and practicing classical music on the piano and the flute, I slipped into my own world. One moment stands out to this day and has proved to be a kind of undercurrent of my life. I was thinking: "How do you create this kind of music?" It seemed the greatest mystery, rather like imagining myself flying to the moon. It wasn't that I dreamed of becoming a composer, there was just this question wanting to be explored. While my life unfolded, I forgot about it entirely.

I studied languages first, and only later music, and finally became a professional musician with a successful career, performing and teaching internationally. After a while, something unexpressed prompted me to start painting and sculpting. Thus began my second career as an artist, before giving up performing altogether. I had achieved all I wanted on the flute.

In the early nineties, after exploring my creativity and artistic expression through art, I felt ready to start creating in music. I envisioned myself recording what I was playing and using that, rather than the traditional method of writing down music. This is indeed possible now, but not in those days. It would take another 10 years before I was able to do this.

Meanwhile, I forgot about music… Until 2001 a former colleague asked me whether I would take over her piano class. She wanted to go on a sabbatical. I had not been active as a classical musician for years and she was asking me to take on a piano class, although I was a flutist. This was quite mysterious. The job proved to be a real gift from heaven: it provided me with the opportunity to participate in an improvisation workshop for pianists, offered through the music school. When I got the flyer, it felt as if I had waited all my life for this moment. I just knew I had to go there.

After the course, I needed to find the right equipment to record my improvisations. I was not familiar with e-pianos, keyboards and synthesisers, but after trying out many different instruments, I finally found the right one. It turned out that the project was on hold again, because I didn't have the means to pay for it.

A year later, my new boyfriend asked me to come

to a trade fair with him. I wasn't really keen on going, but went along because it was something to do together. There, amidst skis and pots and pans, I discovered a stand selling keyboards. Out of the four or five models on display, one of them was the exact one I had chosen a year before. Excited, I showed it to him. And, there and then, he bought it for me!

I now had my instrument, but no clue how to operate it. Life weaved some more magic into this story through the visit of a musician friend, a highly successful violin player. After we had enjoyed a good meal, she surprised me by wanting to play some music together. It had been several years since I had been active as a flutist. Somehow, I mustered the courage to tell her I'd rather play the piano, though I certainly wasn't up to her professional standard on this instrument. After playing a Schubert sonata, my friend suggested I needed to pursue my piano playing. This meant a lot to me. I contacted a violinist I'd worked with, who agreed right away, and she also organised a cellist for us to form a trio.

Overnight, another one of my dreams had come true. I would be playing chamber music on the piano – as a teenager I had seen myself as a pianist, rather than as a flutist. What's more, it was absolutely amazing how well I could play these difficult trios in spite of the fact that I had not practiced all those years. I now played better than ever, and it filled me with tremendous joy.

We began to improvise, using my keyboard, which, apart from helping me gain more experience improvising, also enabled me to get to know the technical aspects of this instrument. After about a year, I wanted to move on to something more professional. The violinist didn't, unfortunately. She was not a professional musician.

Lonely and very disappointed, I sat down at my keyboard, thinking: "I will have to continue on my own". And this is when I finally started composing. A few months later, I completed and published my first CD with my own music. This was 2004.

There were more mysterious threads woven into this story that allowed me "to fly to the moon", composing my own music. But for the purpose of what I'd like to share, let me continue.

Life, and a kind of universal intelligence, had guided me, inspired me and helped my life unfold in a totally unpredictable way, full of magic and mystery, to this point. It had more in store for me.

About 10 years later, I became seriously ill. This made me doubt everything I had done in my life so far. Shouldn't I be healthy and well, having achieved what I had? Having led a creative and spiritual life? I had learned to know myself, I had followed my intuition, and I had co-created with life. What was "missing"?

The answer came from inside: I was meant to learn to love who I am. I had learned to love others unconditionally, but not myself. I now learned that loving myself means loving who I've become, what my life looks like, the choices I've made that brought me here, including everything I don't have. Loving myself has become my daily practice. It has opened up a whole new life. I'm coaching artists, musicians and business people to love themselves and create what matters. I now feel like I belong where I am, most of the time.

Life is making me use a whole new part of my potential that I didn't know I had. It has taken me beyond the moon.

If you feel you could benefit from this approach and are ready to discover your hidden potential, I'd be very happy to support you in this process. There is a course book, and online courses will be published shortly.

Find out more and contact me at www.tessarichter.ch

www.ingramcontent.com/pod-product-compliance
Lightning Source LLC
LaVergne TN
LVHW011016200726
843509LV00011B/1129